LIVERPOOL STREET TO ILFORD

J.E.Connor

Series editor Vic Mitchell

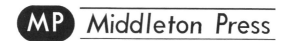

MP Middleton Press

Cover picture : *Liverpool Street in steam days is epitomised by this view of Class B12/3 4-6-0 No. 61577, as she awaits departure from Platform 12 with a good head of steam in January 1958, whilst a Class N7 0-6-2T stands on the adjacent track. (B.P. Pask)*

First published September 1999
First reprint November 2002
Second reprint October 2006

ISBN 1 901706 34 6

© *Middleton Press 1999*

Cover Design Deborah Esher

Published by
        Middleton Press
        Easebourne Lane
        Midhurst
        West Sussex
        GU29 9AZ
Tel: 01730 813169
Fax: 01730 812601
Email: info@middletonpress.co.uk
www.middletonpress.co.uk

Printed & bound by Biddles Ltd, Kings Lynn

CONTENTS

ACKNOWLEDGEMENTS

I should like to thank the various photographers, without whom this volume would not have been possible. I am also grateful to Messrs. J.L. Crook and A.G.W. Garraway who kindly read the proofs.

Lastly, but by no means least, thanks must go to my son Charlie for producing the maps, and to Tricia and Barbie for their general assistance.

GEOGRAPHICAL SETTING

The route is on the northern slope of the lower Thames Valley and crosses the two Thames tributaries - the River Lea west of Stratford and the River Roding on the western approach to Ilford. The boundary between London and Essex was the River Lea until 1965, since which time the entire line has been within the Greater London area. The scale of the maps vary.

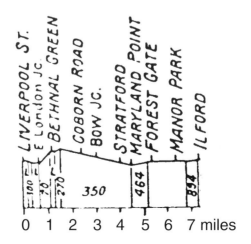

0 1 2 3 4 5 6 7 miles

III

LIVERPOOL STREET TO DEVONSHIRE STREET

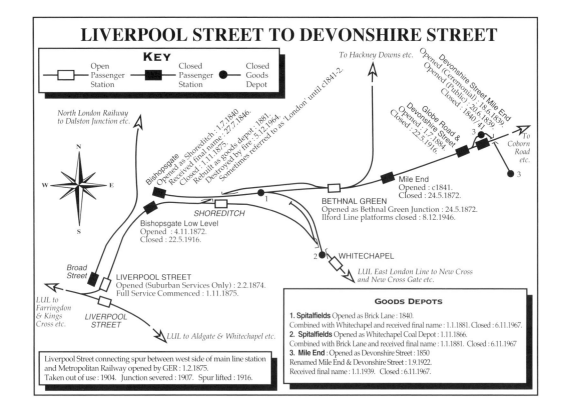

KEY

| Open Passenger Station | Closed Passenger Station | Closed Goods Depot |

GOODS DEPOTS

1. **Spitalfields** Opened as Brick Lane : 1840.
Combined with Whitechapel and received final name : 1.1.1881. Closed : 6.11.1967.
2. **Spitalfields** Opened as Whitechapel Coal Depot : 1.11.1866.
Combined with Brick Lane and received final name : 1.1.1881. Closed : 6.11.1967
3. **Mile End** : Opened as Devonshire Street : 1850
Renamed Mile End & Devonshire Street : 1.9.1922.
Received final name : 1.1.1939. Closed : 6.11.1967.

Liverpool Street connecting spur between west side of main line station and Metropolitan Railway opened by GER : 1.2.1875.
Taken out of use : 1904. Junction severed : 1907. Spur lifted : 1916.

HISTORICAL BACKGROUND

To trace the origins of the line between Liverpool Street and Ilford, we must go back to the 1830s, when the earliest railways to serve London were still in their formative stages.

The route was to link the capital with Norwich, and was initially promoted as the Grand Eastern Counties Railway, but by the time the prospectus was issued, the 'Grand' part of the title had been dropped.

The Bill for its construction was introduced to the House of Commons on 19th February 1836, but received some stiff opposition from both landowners, and the promoters of two rival groups which also wanted to build railways in the area.

Eventually however, all this was overcome, and on 4th July 1836, The Eastern Counties Railway received the Royal Assent.

Initially, the ECR directors were in favour of their line being built in a similar manner to the Great Western Railway, with a track gauge of 7ft 0¼in., but the Engineer, John Braithwaite felt that this would prove too costly, and the idea was eventually dropped. However, as there was initially no intention of making any physical connections with other lines, Braithwaite suggested that it be laid with a non-standard gauge of 5ft, and this was duly accepted.

At the outset, the company was undecided as to the best location for its London terminus, and considered various locations before finally settling for a site adjoining Shoreditch High Street. From here, the line was to be carried on a brick viaduct, which stretched for about a mile and a quarter, and consisted of 160 arches. This proved to be a costly operation, as did a section of embankment

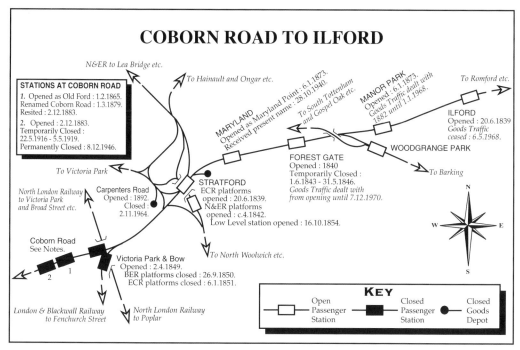

COBORN ROAD TO ILFORD

N&ER to Lea Bridge etc.

To Hainault and Ongar etc.

To Romford etc.

MARYLAND
Opened as Maryland Point : 6.1.1873.
Received present name : 28.10.1940.

To South Tottenham and Gospel Oak etc.

MANOR PARK
Opened : 6.1.1873.
Goods Traffic dealt with 1882 until 1.1.1968.

ILFORD
Opened : 20.6.1839
Goods Traffic
ceased : 6.5.1968.

STATIONS AT COBORN ROAD
1. Opened as Old Ford : 1.2.1865.
Renamed Coborn Road : 1.3.1879.
Resited : 2.12.1883.
2. Opened : 2.12.1883.
Temporarily Closed :
22.5.1916 - 5.5.1919.
Permanently Closed : 8.12.1946.

WOODGRANGE PARK

To Victoria Park

FOREST GATE
Opened : 1840
Temporarily Closed :
1.6.1843 - 31.5.1846.
Goods Traffic dealt with
from opening until 7.12.1970.

To Barking

*North London Railway
to Victoria Park
and Broad Street etc.*

Carpenters Road
Opened : 1892.
Closed :
2.11.1964.

STRATFORD
ECR platforms
opened : 20.6.1839.
N&ER platforms
opened : c.4.1842.
Low Level station opened : 16.10.1854.

N

W   E

S

Coborn Road
See Notes.

To North Woolwich etc.

Victoria Park & Bow
Opened : 2.4.1849.
BER platforms closed : 26.9.1850.
ECR platforms closed : 6.1.1851.

*London & Blackwall Railway
to Fenchurch Street*

*North London Railway
to Poplar*

KEY

| | Open Passenger Station | | Closed Passenger Station | | Closed Goods Depot |

between Bow and Stratford, which was more expensive than anticipated because of the unstable marshy nature of the local terrain, exacerbated by frequent flooding near the bridge over the River Lea. East of Stratford however, things improved and construction became easier.

On the same day that the Eastern Counties received the Royal Assent, another company, the Northern & Eastern Railway also received Parliamentary authority to proceed. This was to connect London with the towns of Bishops Stortford and Hertford, and the promoters originally envisaged that they would have their own City terminus. However, the lack of necessary finance ruled this out, so before construction started the N&ER reached an agreement with the ECR, whereby the two lines joined at Stratford, and both shared the terminus at Shoreditch. The engineer for the Northern & Eastern Railway was Robert Stephenson, and although he was a great advocate of the standard 4ft 8½in gauge, he had to adopt 5ft in order to conform with the ECR.

The first section of the ECR was officially opened between Romford and London on 18th June 1839, but as the premises at Shoreditch were still in the early stages of construction, trains terminated at a temporary station named Devonshire Street, Mile End. The opening ceremony saw a pair of special trains, with locomotives at either end, depart from Devonshire Street, and run parallel with each other to Romford, where invited guests enjoyed a celebratory meal in a nearby

The temporary terminus at Devonshire Street Mile End, from a line drawing by an unknown artist, but possibly contemporary. (J.E. Connor Collection)

marquee.

The terminus at Shoreditch eventually opened on 1st July 1840, although building work still remained unfinished. Devonshire Street was subsequently closed, and eventually demolished. At first the ECR only conveyed passengers, and therefore no freight facilities were provided at Shoreditch. A little later however, the company realised that they were missing out on a very lucrative business, so it constructed a goods station either side of the terminus approach tracks, and named it Brick Lane.

The siting of Shoreditch station proved to be inconvenient for central London, and with the opening of the Northern & Eastern Railway between Stratford and Broxbourne in September 1840, it soon became overcrowded. Its popularity amongst the travelling public was also marred by the fact that it was located very close to one of the East End's most notorious slums - a district known as 'The Old Nichol'. Many of the local inhabitants were criminals, and included burglars, pickpockets and general ruffians. No wonder therefore that armed policemen were on guard at the station during its later stages of construction.

For all the drawbacks associated with Shoreditch station however, traffic on the line began to grow, as the both the ECR and N&ER extended their lines. It therefore soon became obvious that a track gauge of 5ft rather isolated both routes, and impeded their future development, so a decision was made to convert them to standard. The work on this commenced in September 1844, and was completed early the following month.

By this time both companies were effectively under the same management, as from the beginning of 1844, an agreement was reached whereby the ECR leased the Northern & Eastern for a period of 999 years, and took over its operation. The smaller company nevertheless remained nominally independent until 1902.

During these early years, much of the area which eventually became part of London was still rural, and therefore lightly populated. Because of this, the ECR did not initially develop a great deal of suburban traffic.

In 1846, the ECR began to explore the possibility of extending their line into the City, and considered sites at Farringdon

EASTERN COUNTIES.

Shoreditch to Brentwood. Departure from	8 30 a.m.	11 a.m.	2 p.m.	3 p.m.	4¼ p.m.	5 p.m.	6½ p.m.	7¾ p.m.
Shoreditch	8 30	11 0	2 0	3 0	4 15	5 0	6 30	*7 45
Mile End	8 34	11 4	2 4	3 4	..	..	..	..
Stratford	8 41	11 11	2 11	3 11	4 25	5 10	6 40	7 55
Forest Gate	..	..	..	..	4 29	..	..	..
Ilford	8 50	11 20	2 20	3 20	4 35	5 19	6 49	8 4
Romford	9 1	11 31	2 31	3 31	4 46	5 30	7 0	8 15

Brentwood to Shoreditch. Departure from	8¾ a.m.	9¾ a.m.	10¾ a.m.	12½ a.m.	3½ p.m.	5½ p.m.	6¾ p.m.	7¾ p.m.
Brentwood	8 45	9 45	10 45	12 30	3 30	5 30	6 30	*7 45
Romford	9 0	10 0	11 0	12 45	3 45	5 45	6 45	8 0
Ilford	9 11	10 11	11 11	12 56	3 56	5 56	6 56	8 11
Forest Gate	9 17	..	..	..	..	..	..	..
Stratford	9 21	10 19	11 19	1 4	4 4	6 4	7 4	8 19
Mile End	9 28	..	..	1 11	..	6 11	7 11	..

On Sundays from Shoreditch at 9 and 10 a.m., and 2, 3, 6¼ p.m.—From Brentwood at 8¾, and 10 a.m. and 1¼, 4½, and 6¼ p.m.

* These trains will only run in the months of May, June, July, Aug. and Sept.
Fares.—London to Brentwood, first class 3s. 6d., second 2s. 6d., third 2s.

1841

Street, Finsbury Square and Fore Street. However, none of these proposals were to materialise, so for the time being at least, the Company had to make the best of what they already had.

An important development came in 1847, when the ECR transferred their locomotive works from Romford to Stratford, and erected 300 houses nearby to accommodate the workforce. Because the nineteenth century entrepreneur George Hudson was now chairman of the Eastern Counties Railway, the district was dubbed 'Hudson's Town', and continued to be referred to locally as 'New Town' until recent times. The development was not without its critics however, as a contemporary journalist wrote in sentimental vein *"A city smokes where cornfields smiled before."*

The advent of the London Tilbury & Southend Railway in 1854 brought additional traffic to the western end of the route, as LTSR trains initially used ECR metals until diverging onto their own system east of Forest Gate. Some LTSR services ran into Bishopsgate, whilst others used Fenchurch Street as their London terminus. To reach the latter, they operated over the Blackwall Extension Railway from Bow Junction, and an additional down line had to be laid between there and Stratford to convey trains from Fenchurch Street.

With the various lines serving East Anglia becoming inter-dependant on each other, it was perhaps only a matter of time before an amalgamation took place. This occurred following a Parliamentary Act of 7th August 1862, when the ECR was grouped with various provincial companies to form the Great Eastern Railway.

One of the earliest tasks ahead of the new company concerned the replacement of the terminus at Bishopsgate. The directors therefore suggested that a completely new station should be built, and the premises at Bishopsgate be converted into a goods depot.

The old Finsbury Circus proposal was dusted off and revived, but there was too much local opposition, so it was abandoned. Therefore a new location had to be found, and the choice fell on Liverpool Street. The Parliamentary authority to go ahead was received in 1865, but it was not until 2nd February 1874 that it was possible to open the first section of the new terminus. Two years earlier had seen a great expansion of lines in the Great Eastern suburban area, with routes stretching northwards from Bethnal Green to serve embryonic residential districts such as Edmonton and Walthamstow. All this brought additional strain on the existing terminal facilities, although a degree of relief was afforded when the Liverpool Street extension was opened as far as a new Low Level station at Bishopsgate on 4th November 1872.

Walthamstow and Enfield trains began using Liverpool Street station from 2nd February 1874, but because constructional work was still incomplete a full service could not begin until 1st November 1875. Once the entire station was up and running, there was no need to retain the old terminus at Bishopsgate, so it was closed, and subsequently used for goods traffic.

Initially there were four tracks on the approach to Liverpool Street, with the pair serving the east side used by main line trains, and the other two by suburban services.

During the 1870s, the urbanisation of the area served by the line took on a new rapidity, and erstwhile rural backwaters such as Forest Gate were fast becoming engulfed in a sea of bricks and mortar. Traffic continued to grow, and the existing tracks began to get congested. To help remedy this, a fourth track was added between Bow Junction and Stratford in 1877, and two separate goods lines were laid from Stratford to Maryland Point, but more work was obviously still required.

Quadrupling between Bethnal Green Junction and Bow Junction was authorised in 1876, and six years later powers were obtained to do likewise from Maryland Point to Ilford.

Also in 1876, the GER obtained Parliamentary authority to enlarge the former Bishopsgate terminus site, and rebuild the premises so that they were more suited to handling freight. The work proved lengthy, and had to be done with the minimum disruption to existing traffic, but the new facilities, albeit unfinished, were eventually brought into use on 1st January 1881.

Meanwhile, the job of quadrupling the main line continued, although as the London end required the viaduct to be widened, this proved both lengthy and costly. The first section, from James Street (near Globe Road) to Bow Junction was ready by 1884, but the stretch between James Street and Bethnal Green station took an additional seven years. At the time, the formation west of Bethnal Green was provided with two additional tracks, which therefore increased the number of roads approaching the terminus to six. Work on the formation east of Maryland Point was also progressing, and the quadrupling was completed over the three-year period of 1892-1895.

Another task to be tackled around the same time, was the enlargement of Liverpool Street station, by the provision of eight additional platforms to the east of the original premises. Work commenced in 1890, and the new East Side extension were brought into use on 2nd April 1894.

Much of the site used for enlarging Liverpool Street had previously been occupied by housing, and Parliament insisted that the GER had to provide alternative accommodation for the displaced tenants at low fixed rents. 137 people were rehoused in existing properties, but for the remaining 600, the company erected blocks of flats in Fieldgate Street, Winchester Street and Quaker Street.

At the time of the quadrupling, various station changes took place, but platforms were initially only provided on the slow lines. This may have made sense at some of the places served, but led to operational problems, so in 1898 and 1900, through line platforms were brought into use at Ilford

and Stratford respectively.

With very intensive suburban services now in operation, the GER began to seek more efficient means of working, and in the early years of the twentieth century explored the possibilities of electrification. Because of the continuing problem of overcrowding on the existing tracks, the company also considered the construction of a deep level tube line to virtually parallel the route to Goodmayes, and during 1913 some detailed reports were made to examine the best course which this could take. Three routes from the City were considered, with two beneath the existing line to Stratford, and the other beneath Whitechapel Road. The latter would have more or less followed the existing Whitechapel & Bow Railway of 1902, and it was felt that this option would meet with a great deal of opposition, so it would probably be best forgotten. The Great Eastern tube would have been nine and a quarter miles long, and could possibly have made an end-on connection with the Central London Railway at Liverpool Street. However, all these plans proved to be purely hypothetical, as the scheme was never to materialise, although many years later another part of the Great Eastern suburban system would be incorporated into the tube network, as we shall see.

A company report of 1913 noted that the GER were constantly receiving complaints from passengers regarding overcrowding on peak-hour Ilford line trains, but although the outer suburban district remained buoyant, traffic in the inner area was being badly eroded by tramway competition.

After World War 1, the possibility of electrification was again discussed, with consideration being given to much of the suburban system. A report dated September 1918 stated that benefits brought by electric traction would increase the traffic potential at Liverpool Street by at least 50%, but to enable this to work efficiently various expensive alterations to the permanent way would have been necessary, so the company had to think again.

Instead of electrification, the GER decided to completely revise its method of working at terminal stations, and in 1920 introduced what was described as *"The last word in steam operated suburban services"* on the Hackney Downs group of lines. Locomotive working became slicker, and brightly coloured strips were painted above carriage windows to provide instant identification of the accommodation on offer. This greatly cut down on the amount of time lost at stations, as passengers wanting First Class had only to look for a yellow stripe, whilst those requiring Second would look for blue.

The previous year, The Original Dixieland Jazz Band had arrived from America to appear in the musical revue *Joy Bells* at the London Hippodrome, and although they only made a single appearance in the show, their influence was such on popular culture that the word 'jazz' was now on everyone's lips. This was not just confined to music, and it soon became synonymous with anything loud and garish. As the bright colours employed to denote class of travel were deemed 'jazzy', the contemporary media came up with the term ' Jazz Service', which continued in use for a while, and was even briefly re-introduced as a branding for suburban trains in the 1980s. A similar re-organisation was planned for the Ilford line, but by now the independence of the GER was in its final days.

Much of Britain's railway system was in a run-down condition after World War 1, and this led to The Railway Act of 1921. This was actually implemented from 1st January 1923, when the majority of companies were merged to form four large groups. Under this arrangement, the Great Eastern ceased to exist as a separate entity and became part of the London & North Eastern Railway.

Despite the success of 'The Jazz Service', the LNER were still tempted by the benefits of electrification, but all ideas in this direction were to remain moribund until 1935 when a completely new scheme was announced. The route between Liverpool Street and Shenfield was to be served by electric trains provided by the LNER, but that which linked central London with Ongar and Hainault was to be incorporated into the London Passenger Transport Board's Central Line.

Work on the section to be retained by the LNER was duly started, but progress was slow as it was to be completed without undue interruption of existing traffic. The existing local and through lines would exchange roles as far as Ilford, where a new flyover would be constructed enabling them to revert. This was not the only major civil engineering work to be undertaken however, as the project at Stratford included connections with the Central Line, which was to be extended in tunnel from its existing terminus at Liverpool Street, then after surfacing briefly at the station, plunge down into another section of tube which linked with the existing Ongar and Hainault routes near Leyton.

Work was suspended during World War ll, and therefore completion was heavily delayed. Tube trains finally reached Stratford in December 1946, and were extended to Leytonstone in the following May, but electrification of the Shenfield line remained unfinished until 1949.

From 1st January 1948 the railway network was nationalised, and the line became part of the Eastern Region of British Railways.

The new electric units therefore entered traffic under BR ownership, although they had been designed prior to nationalisation. The coach interiors were in some ways reminiscent of contemporary Underground vehicles, and were equipped with strap hangers for the convenience of passengers who were unable to find a vacant seat during the morning and evening peaks. Diagrammatic system maps were positioned inside each vehicle, and these were again similar in concept to those employed by London Transport. The earliest of these included the section between Stratford and Fenchurch Street, which was originally intended for electrification, but closed to passengers from 7th November 1949, and subsequently only used by public services as a diversionary route.

The Liverpool Street-Shenfield electrification was initially powered at 1500 volts dc, and remained as such when the overhead wires were continued to Chelmsford in 1956. However, soon afterwards, as further extensions were being planned, British Railways decided to standardise on the 25kV system, and the route was duly converted in November 1960.

Since then, the Ilford line has witnessed various other changes, including the rebuilding of Liverpool Street, and an intensive programme of resignalling, but although much has altered since steam days, there is still plenty to interest the railway minded traveller on this fascinating journey through east London.

With the break-up of the nationalised network in the 1990s, Railtrack became responsible for infrastructure, and train operation was taken over by three different companies. Norwich services were worked by Anglia Railways, whilst trains on the Chingford and Enfield lines were provided by West Anglia Great Northern. On 4th December 1996, FirstBus plc began working local trains on the Liverpool Street - Southend and Colchester / Ipswich routes, which includes the section to Ilford. The company have adopted the title 'Great Eastern Railway', and therefore have revived a historic name after an absence of over seventy years.

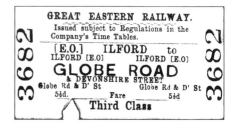

PASSENGER SERVICES

To catalogue the development of these in detail would be impossible without producing a dull list of figures, so only a basic outline is given here.

In the 1840s and 50s the service on the Ilford line was largely of a main line nature, as the eastern suburbs beyond Stratford were slow to develop.

In later years however, as urbanisation spread, more and more trains used the line, with local services reaching a peak around the end of the nineteenth century.

In addition to destinations on the GER, and to a lesser extent, the LTSR, it was also possible to travel from Liverpool Street to stations in what was then suburban Surrey by way of the East London line, although workings such as these had gone by the time of the 1923 grouping.

World War ll ended through services between Liverpool Street and the North Woolwich group of lines, whilst post-war changes saw the Ongar and Hainault routes being swallowed up by London Transport.

Following electrification in 1949, the majority of suburban services terminated at Shenfield, although some reversed at intermediate stations such as Gidea Park.

The overhead wires were later extended deep into the Essex heartland and beyond, resulting in the destinations of outer suburban trains becoming even further afield. In general terms, by the 1990s, stopping services were working out to Shenfield, with semi-fasts travelling to Southminster, Southend Victoria, Braintree and Colchester.

LIVERPOOL STREET

1. We start our journey by standing in Liverpool Street itself, and looking across the road to the station frontage. Almost directly opposite are the gates which separated the public right of way from the inclined approach, whilst all around us is the hustle and bustle of London in the early twentieth century. Most of the buildings seen here date from 1875, although the section on the extreme left was an afterthought which was added in 1883. The design for the station was attributed to the engineer Edward Wilson, although it seems likely that an architect may have been employed as well. The imposing clock tower, which prior to 1883 marked the corner of the premises, once stood to a height of 150 feet, but this was reduced when its pinnacle was removed following war damage in 1941. The other large block, which can be seen a little to the right of centre, was 90 feet high, and accommodated the main booking office. The close proximity of the North London Railway terminus at Broad Street is emphasised by the LNWR sign referring to goods facilities which is partially visible to our left above the horse-drawn goods vehicle, and delightful trader's tricycle. (Lens of Sutton)

C.E.R. PLAN OF LIVERPOOL STREET STATION

(Railway Magazine November 1899)

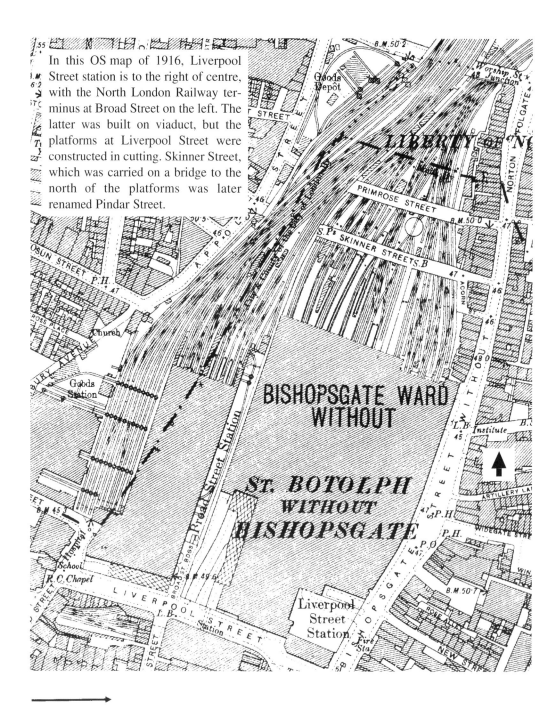

In this OS map of 1916, Liverpool Street station is to the right of centre, with the North London Railway terminus at Broad Street on the left. The latter was built on viaduct, but the platforms at Liverpool Street were constructed in cutting. Skinner Street, which was carried on a bridge to the north of the platforms was later renamed Pindar Street.

3. Looking down from the footbridge onto the East Side concourse, as it appeared about five years after completion. This part of the station, which comprised eight new platforms was designed by W.N. Ashbee, head of the GER architectural section, and was brought into public use on 2nd April 1894. Platforms 11 and 12 were designated for main line arrivals, as was No.13, although the latter was also used by down Colchester stopping trains. Nos.14-18 served destinations on the Southend and East London lines, together with Barking on the LTSR, which was reached by way of Forest Gate Junction. (Lens of Sutton)

2. Here can be seen the two main line platforms, which formed the station's eastern boundary until the premises were extended in 1894. To our left is platform 9, which was accessed directly from the main line booking hall, whilst to the right is No.10. The tracks serving these, together with one of the centre roads, were extended at their terminal end beneath the Great Eastern Hotel, which was completed in May 1884. There was once an overnight departmental train from Stratford, which brought in various supplies, and returned with hotel refuse. The footbridge seen in the middle distance was added in 1894, and led to the new East Side entrance in Bishopsgate. (Lens of Sutton)

4. Opened in 1894, the East Side entrance is viewed here from Bishopsgate in the 1980s. Together with an adjoining railway office block and the Great Eastern Hotel, this differed from the original part of the station in that it was constructed from red brick as opposed to white. Both doorways led onto the footbridge, but the one to the left also served a booking office. (B.P. Pask)

5. We now stand at the north end of the station and witness main line arrivals in pre-grouping days. In this view Class D56 4-4-0 No.1821 is passing beneath Primrose Street bridge with the 3.50pm train from Southend on 28th July 1909. The locomotive had not long entered traffic, having made her first run a few days earlier on 23rd July with the 9.04am excursion from Liverpool Street to Southend, and when recorded here her paintwork was shining to perfection. (K. Nunn/LCGB)

6. Moving back to the station itself, a large boilered Class T19 2-4-0 No.770 is seen arriving with the 2.45pm train from Cambridge, having just passed beneath Pindar Street bridge. To the right stands one of the once ubiquitous 0-4-4Ts used on suburban services. (K. Nunn/LCGB)

7. Still at the station's north end, a small boilered Class T19 2-4-0 No.1030 is awaiting departure around 1903. In the background can be seen the North London Railway viaduct, with a characteristic rake of four-wheeled coaches standing in front of Broad Street No.1 signal box. (R. Blencowe Collection)

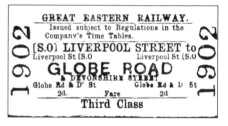

8. In 1928, Mr. H.N. (later Sir Nigel) Gresley introduced his B17 Class 4-6-0s, primarily for working services on the Great Eastern Section. Here No. 2816 *Fallodon* stands on one of the servicing roads at Liverpool Street in the 1930s, alongside the inclined approach from Pindar Street, which was used by taxicabs accessing the station, and separated the original premises of 1874/5 from the extension of 1894. (Lens of Sutton)

9. The cab road provided an excellent spot for watching movements around the station, and was therefore popular with enthusiasts. In this view we are looking over the wall, and see Class B2 4-6-0 No. 61671 *Royal Sovereign* which had previously worked in on an up service. No. 61671 was at one time regularly used on royal trains, and was invariably kept very clean. In 1950, she was outshopped from Darlington Works in LNER green with the BR emblem on her tender, as seen here. This livery proved fairly short-lived however, and she was later repainted in the darker shade of green adopted as standard by British Railways. (Photomatic)

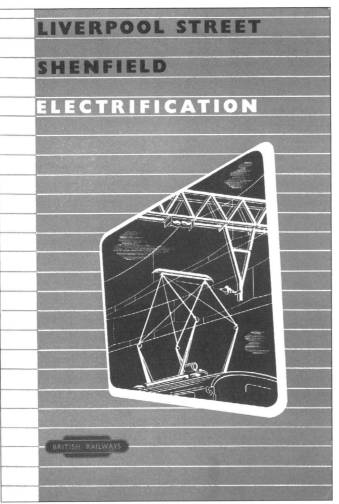

Cover of a booklet published by The Railway Executive (ER) describing the newly electrified route to Shenfield. (J.E. Connor Collection)

Extract from the BR timetable issued 26th September 1949. Electric trains began working on the line from this date, but the full service to and from Shenfield was not introduced until well over a month later later on 7th November.

LIVERPOOL STREET, FENCHURCH STREET, STRATFORD, ILFORD, ROMFORD, BRENTWOOD & WARLEY, SHENFIELD & HUTTON AND CHELMSFORD

WEEKDAYS—continued

THROUGH TRAINS FROM LIVERPOOL STREET OR FENCHURCH STREET ARE SHOWN IN BOLD TYPE

B Third Class only
B Saturdays only. Calls at Shenfield & Hutton to take up passengers only

SO Saturdays only
SX Saturdays excepted

35

10. On the East Side of the station Class A5 4-6-2T No. 69830 awaits departure with a train for Southend in 1951. The wires erected for the Shenfield electrification scheme can be seen above, and one of the electric units is just visible to our left. No. 69830 was built to a Great Central design by Hawthorn Leslie in September 1925, and was drafted to the Great Eastern Section when a temporary lack of turning facilities at Liverpool Street brought about an urgent need for tank locomotives to work the Southend services. (J.E. Connor Collection)

11. The reason why there was a temporary lack of turning facilities was because the locomotive turntable required lengthening so that it could accommodate the new BR Standard Class 7 Pacifics which were about to be introduced. Here it can be seen a little later in the decade, with Class B1 4-6-0 No. 61052 in the process of being turned. Behind her is the Pindar Street bridge, which had been rebuilt from its earlier form seen in photograph No. 6 in connection with the Shenfield Electrification project. (A. Ingram)

12. In the Spring of 1951 three Southern Region Bulleid 4-6-2s were transferred to Stratford. Whilst they were there, the new Standard Class 7 Pacifics were unexpectedly taken out of traffic following a mechanical failure, and the Bulleid locos got the chance to prove their worth. In this view we can enjoy the sight of 'Battle of Britain' class No. 34057 'Biggin Hill' setting out with a down express, as a BR Standard Pacific awaits departure from the adjoining platform. (K. Nunn/LCGB)

13. Standing on platform 10 we look towards No. 9, and see Class J69/1 0-6-0T No. 68619, and Class N7/4 0-6-2T No. 69614, which were both employed on station pilot duties during the 1950s and early 1960s. These locomotives were always well cared-for at Stratford shed, and were invariably in immaculate condition. (Photomatic)

14. Once their early teething troubles had been remedied, the BR Class 7 Pacifics, or *Britannias* as they were more familiarly known, became firm favourites with GE line locomotive crews and enthusiasts alike. Here No. 70012 *John of Gaunt* prepares to depart with an express from platform 9, as station pilot No. 68619 waits for her next duty. In 1959, this engine was painted in a version of GER dark ultramarine, and soon received the nickname of *The Blue Angel* after Josef Von Sternberg's famous 1930 film starring Marlene Dietrich. (R.A. Panting)

15. Enthusiasts watch from the cab road as a Brush Type 2 diesel departs amidst a thick cloud of fumes. These locomotives first entered traffic in 1957, and a number of them were allocated to Stratford for GE line workings. (P.H. Groom)

16. Shafts of light stream through openings in the wall which divided the original 1870s part of the station from the 1894 addition. We are standing on the cab road between platforms 10 and 11 in 1981, and are looking towards its southern exit which led into Liverpool Street itself. (J.E. Connor)

17. This 1980s view looks down upon the East Side concourse from the footbridge which led from the Bishopsgate entrance. As can be seen, the bridge did not take a direct course at this point, but followed the station walls. The attractive stilted gazebo to the left was once a refreshment room, but in later years was adapted for railway purposes. Directly ahead is a chemists shop and fruit kiosk, both of which boast fascias in the unmistakable style of the 1930s, whilst between these is a stairway leading to the LT Central Line. (J.E. Connor)

18. From the same footbridge, but later in the decade, we look northwards and see rebuilding work in progress. The East Side trainshed featured here was subsequently demolished, and replaced by a new flat deck roof which supports commercial premises above. (B.P. Pask)

19.   Standing on the elevated walkway, we look west, and watch passengers milling around the concourse in 1999. The rebuilding was completed in December 1991 and cost £162 million. It was financed by closing the adjoining Broad Street station, and selling its site for redevelopment. (J.E. Connor)

20.   Class 86 electric locomotive No. 86217 *Halley's Comet* stands beneath the 1875 trainshed after arrival from Norwich in 1993. Unlike its counterpart on the East Side, this historic roof was retained during the rebuilding, and has been renovated. (J.E. Connor)

BISHOPSGATE HIGH LEVEL

The original Eastern Counties Railway terminus at Bishopsgate is shown near the bottom of this OS map from 1872. The station was opened on 1st July 1840 with the name 'Shoreditch', although the company often referred to it simply as 'London' for the first two or three years. The close proximity of the notorious slum district around Old Nichol's Street can be seen to the north. In an attempt to make the station sound closer to the City, it was renamed Bishopsgate from 27th July 1846, but this did little to improve its public image. Our map shows the station in its final form, with additional tracks on the north side of the site, which were used by suburban services.

21. The terminus at Bishopsgate was rebuilt in the late 1840s, when it was provided with an Italianate main building by the architect Sancton Wood. The frontage as it appeared around 1865 can be admired in this view taken from the opposite side of Shoreditch High Street. When first opened, the station was partially hidden from the road by a row of old houses, but these were removed after a few years, and replaced by the single storey shops seen here. Passengers arriving by horse-drawn carriage would be taken up the slope to the left, and set-down beneath the awning, whilst those who came on foot would ascend one of the two frontal stairways. Most of the ground floor accommodation was used for passenger facilities, and the second storey housed the offices of the Eastern Counties and Northern & Eastern Railways in the early years. (British Rail)

LONDON, STRATFORD & CHELMSFORD, to COLCHESTER & BURY.—Eastern Counties.

Miles.	Down. From Shoreditch Station.	Week Days. 1 2 3 gov.	mail, 1 2cl.	1 2 3 clss.	1 &2 qck.	1 2 3 clss	1&2 cls.	1 2 3 cls.	1 & 2 mail.	1 2 3 class.	Sundays. 1 2 3 gov.	1 2 3 class.	1 2 3 cls.	1 2 3 cls.	1 & 2 mail.	Fares. 1stcl.	2d.cl.	3 cls.	gov.
		morn	morn	aft	aft.	aft.	aft	aft	aft	aft.	mrn	morn	aft	aft	aft	s. d.	s. d.	s. d.	s. d.
—	**LONDON**..dep.	8 10	11 0	1 30	3 30	4 20	5 30	6 30	8 30	10 15	8 0	10 15	2 45	6 0	8 30	..	..	..	..
1	Mile End	8 13	..	1 33	..	4 23	..	..	..	..	8 3	10 18	2 48	6 3	..	0 4	0 3	0 2	0 1
2½	Victoria Prk & Bow	8 17	..	1 37	..	4 27	..	6 35	..	..	8 7	10 22	2 52	6 7	..	0 4	0 3	0 2	0 2
3¾	**Stratford**	8 25	11 10	1 45	..	4 33	5 41	6 40	8 40	10 30	8 15	10 28	2 58	6 13	8 40	0 6	0 4	0 3	0 3
5	Forest Gate	8 30	..	1 50	..	4 37	5 45	6 44	..	Stopping at Mile End when required: also on Sundays.	8 20	10 31	3 1	6 17	..	1 0	0 8	0 5	0 5
7	Ilford	8 38	11 17	1 58	3 46	4 44	5 52	6 51	8 46		8 30	10 37	3 7	6 26	8 46	1 4	1 0	0 7	0 7
12	Romford	8 52	11 28	2 12	3 58	4 55	6 7	7 8	8 54		8 46	10 52	3 22	6 39	8 54	2 6	1 9	1 0	1 0
17¾	Brentwood	9 7	11 45	2 30	4 11	5 10	6 23	7 25	9 11		9 6	10 10	3 40	6 55	9 11	3 9	2 9	1 9	1 5½
19¾	Shenfield	9 14	..	—	..	—	..	7 32	..		9 13	—	3 46	7 1	..	4 3	3 3	2 0	1 7½
23¼	Ingatestone	9 23	11 56	..	4 24	..	6 40	7 42	9 35		9 23	..	3 55	7 12	9 35	5 3	4 0	3 0	1 11
29¼	**Chelmsford**..	9 40	12 10	..	4 37	..	6 55	7 53	9 48		9 38	..	4 30	7 27	9 48	6 9	5 3	4 0	2 5
38¼	Witham	10 5	12 20	..	4 54	..	7 22	—	10 13		10 4	..	—	7 51	10 13	9 0	6 9	5 3	3 2
41¾	Kelvedon........	10 17	12 40	..	5 3	..	7 33	..	10 23		10 15	..	..	8 2	10 23	9 9	7 9	6 0	3 5½
46¼	Marks Tey Jun...	10 30	12 50	..	5 16	..	7 44	..	..		10 26	..	..	8 13	..	11 0	8 9	6 9	3 10
51¼	**Colchester** arr	10 50	1 10	..	5 35	..	8 5	..	10 49		10 55	..	..	8 40	10 49	12 6	10 0	7 3	4 3
68	**Ipswich**	11 50	1 50	..	6 20	..	8 56	..	11 39		..	..	..	..	11 39	..	..	..	..
94½	**Bury St.Edm.**	1 15	3 0	..	7 35	..	..	..	..		..	..	..	..	..	..	..	..	..

Miles.	For stations between Bury and Colchester, p 33.	Week Days. 1 &2 mail	1 2 3 cls.	1& 2 qck.	1 2 3 clss.	1 & 2 mail.	1& 2 cls.	1 2 3 class.	1 2 3 gov.	Sundays. 1& 2 mail	1 2 3 gov.	1 2 3 class.	1 2 3 class.	1 2 3 cls.	Fares fm Colchester 1st.cl	2d.cl.	3 cl.	gov
		mrn	mrn	mrn	morn	morn	aft.	aft.	aft	mrn	morn	aft	aft	aft	s. d.	s. d.	s. d.	s. d.
—	**Bury St.Ed**	..	..	..	..	8†10	12 15	..	4 50	..	..	..	..	..	..	..	..	..
26½	**Ipswich** ..	1 20	..	7 0	..	9 30	1 30	..	6 0	1 20	..	..	..	..	..	..	..	..
43¼	**Colchester**	2 11	*	7 45	..	10 25	2 20	..	6 45	2 11	9 30	5‡15	..	..	..	..	..	..
48¼	Marks Tey ..	..	..	7 56	..	10 35	2 29	..	7 3	..	9 41	5 25	..	..	1 3	1 0	0 9	0 5
52¾	Kelvedon ..	2 37	..	8 9	..	10 45	2 41	..	7 15	2 37	9 52	5 38	..	..	2 3	1 6	1 0	0 9½
56¼	Witham......	2 47	..	8 29	..	11 7	2 51	..	7 25	2 47	10 7	5 47	p.m.	..	2 9	2 3	1 9	1 1
65¼	**Chelmsfrd.**	3 12	7 40	8 45	..	11 30	3 8	..	7 50	3 12	10 32	6 11	8 0	..	4 9	3 9	2 9	1 10
71¼	Ingatestone ..	3 26	7 55	8 58	..	11 45	3 25	..	8 5	3 26	10 49	6 30	8 20	..	7 0	5 0	3 9	2 4
74¾	Shenfield	..	8 7	9 7	..	..	..	..	8 14	..	11 2	..	8 30	..	7 9	6 0	4 3	2 6½
76¾	Brentwood ..	3 41	8 15	9 13	10 35	11 58	3 39	5 20	8 20	3 41	11 8	6 45	8 35	9 0	8 3	6 3	4 6	2 8½
82½	Romford	3 57	8 32	9 30	10 50	12 13	3 55	5 30	8 35	3 57	11 24	7 3	8 53	9 15	9 3	7 3	5 3	3 3
87½	Ilford	4 12	8 43	9 43	11 4	12 27	4 8	5 40	8 49	4 12	11 39	7 16	9 8	9 29	11 0	8 6	6 3	3 8
89½	Forest Gate .	..	8 49	..	11 12	..	4 13	5 47	8 55	..	11 47	7 22	9 14	9 37	11 9	9 3	6 9	3 10
90¾	**Stratford**..	4 22	8 54	9 55	11 17	12 36	4 19	5 51	9 3	4 22	11 57	7 25	9 22	9 42	11 9	9 3	6 9	3 11½
92	Vic.Park&Bow	..	9 0	..	11 25	..	..	5 56	9 10	..	12 5	..	9 32	..	12 6	10 0	7 3	4 0½
93½	Mile End ..	..	..	..	11 29	Wed.	..	6 2	9 13	..	12 8	..	9 36	9 52	12 6	10 0	7 3	4 2
94½	**London**..arr	4 30	9 10	10 5	11 35	12 50	4 35	6 15	9 20	4 30	12 15	7 40	9 45	10 0	12 6	10 0	7 3	4 3

† 3rd class mail from Bury. ‡ 1 & 2 only from Bury.

* From Colchester on Mondays at 6 45 a.m. calling at all Stations except Mile End. 1st and 2nd class Day Tickets issued to London. The Black lines under certain arrivals show that those trains run no further.

March 1850

22. The interior of Bishopsgate terminus in December 1850, shows how busy it could be around Christmas time. A train has just arrived, and staff are unloading luggage which had been carried, stagecoach style, on the carriage roofs. As built by the engineer John Braithwaite, the station had just two platforms, with the most northerly being used for departures and the other for arrivals. These were protected from the elements by a three-span corrugated iron roof, supported by the side walls and two rows of cast-iron columns. (Illustrated London News)

BISHOPSGATE GOODS

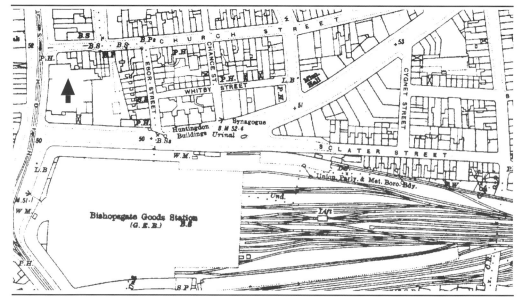

With Liverpool Street fully functioning, Bishopsgate was of no further use for passenger traffic, so it closed from 1st November 1875. It was then used as a goods depot, but its layout was far from ideal, so it was extensively rebuilt in 1881. Before this could be done it was necessary for the GER to obtain Parliamentary Authority as several adjoining streets were scheduled to disappear under the new development. (OS Map 1914)

23. Looking across Shoreditch High Street to Bishopsgate goods depot in pre-grouping days, it can be seen that nothing has survived of the old passenger terminus after the rebuilding of 1881. The depot had facilities on three levels, with a basement located within the arches, tracks on the viaduct, and a large warehouse above. (Lens of Sutton)

24. Here we look west across the yard, towards the main depot building. In front of this, just left of centre, is a wagon hoist which connected the tracks seen here with those at basement level, whilst to the right is a small shed used for Continental traffic. (British Rail)

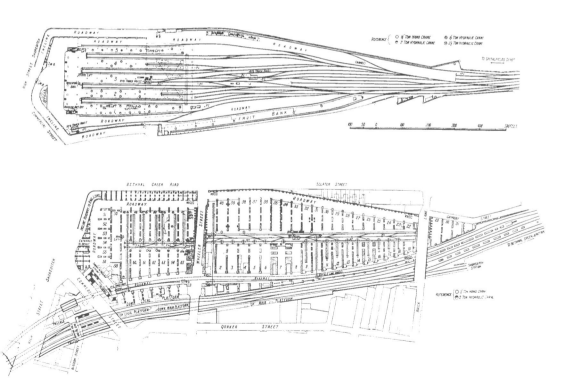

The upper level is shown at the top, with the basement below. Towards the base of the lower diagram the lines serving Liverpool Street are shown, with Bishopsgate Low Level passenger station at the bottom left. (Railway Magazine March 1933)

BISHOPSGATE LOW LEVEL

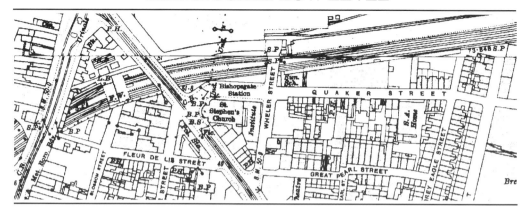

At the top of this OS map of 1916 can be seen the station, which was opened on 4th November 1872, and used as a terminus by certain suburban trains until it was possible to open part of Liverpool Street in February 1874. The station building straddled the tracks at the west end, and was accessed by means of two passageways which linked Shoreditch High Street with Commercial Street. Stairways connected the booking hall with the down local platform, and an island which served both the up local and down through lines. There was also an up through platform, but this was staggered to the east of Wheeler Street, and had its own separate access by means of a doorway on the north side of Quaker Street. When the formation was widened, two further platforms were opened on 5th April 1891 to serve the new West Side suburban tracks beneath the goods depot, and at the same time an additional booking office was opened within an existing arch on the east side of Commercial Street.

25. Class M15 2-4-2T No. 577 passes the up through platform on 9th May 1912, with the 1.45pm train from Liverpool Street to Gallions. Through the haze of smoke, we can just see Wheeler Street bridge in the distance, whilst to the right is a section of the viaduct which served Bishopsgate goods depot. (K. Nunn/LCGB)

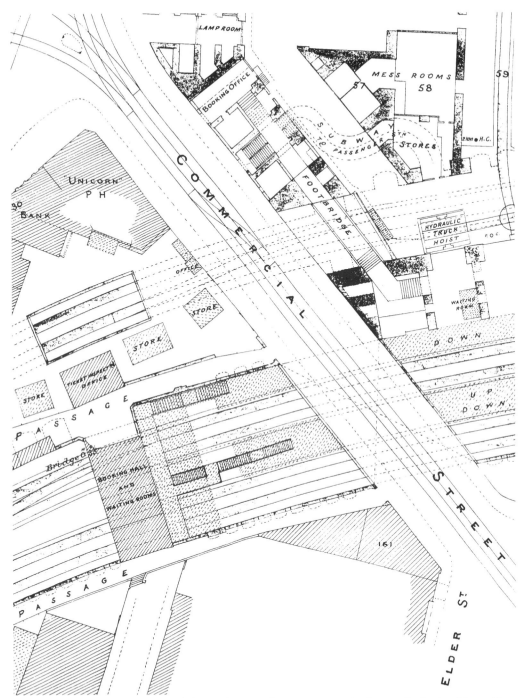

This plan shows the location of the various station entrances. At the top is the booking office opened in 1891, which was situated in one of the arches beneath the goods depot. Tickets issued from here generally show the station's name followed by the initials 'CSO' which stood for 'Commercial Street Office'. Further down, to the left, is the original entrance, which was reached by means of the passageways linking Commercial Street and Shoreditch High Street. The tracks seen running along Commercial Street formed part of the London tramway network. (G. Kenworthy Collection)

26. A fine view of Bishopsgate Low Level, looking towards Liverpool Street, shortly before closure. The island serving the up local and down through lines features prominently, and displays the type of awning employed on many GER suburban stations of the 1870s. The signal box was located towards the country end of the down local platform, and it is possible that the photographer was leaning from this when the picture was taken. The bridge seen in the middle distance is that which carries Commercial Street. (British Rail)

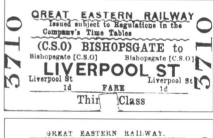

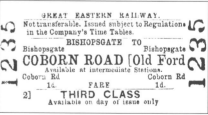

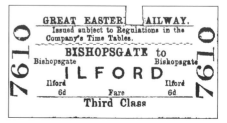

27. The station closed as a wartime economy measure on 22nd May 1916, and never reopened. It was subsequently largely demolished, although some parts of it survived. This 1930s view is looking east from beneath the Wheeler Street bridge, towards the former up through platform, which by then had lost its awning. The GER Quaker Street stables, very necessary in the days before motorised road transport, loom above, whilst to the left stand Great Eastern Buildings, two parallel blocks of model dwellings erected by the railway in 1890 to rehouse those made homeless by the enlargement of Liverpool Street. (British Rail)

28. The old up through line platform survived in 1999, and still retained its stairway at the London end. In this 1995 picture a Class 321 EMU is passing, as it heads towards Liverpool Street on an up service from Southend. This type of electric stock, introduced in 1988, took over all Southend workings from the earlier slam-door Class 307 units in 1990. (J.E. Connor)

29. From the window of a train, we look towards Liverpool Street in the early 1990s, and see the old up through line platform in the distance. On the right is the covered way which was built beneath Bishopsgate goods depot to accommodate the two additional West Side suburban lines when the formation was widened in 1891. Parts of the platforms erected to serve these at Bishopsgate Low Level still survived, although being in the gloomy confines of the covered way, they were less clearly seen from a passing train, than the one on the up through. (B.P. Pask)

G. E. R.

—

Bishopsgate

30. A short distance to the east of the up through line platform at Bishopsgate Low Level was East London Junction, where the East London Railway diverged towards Whitechapel and New Cross. Standing just west of the junction, there is a good view of the signal box to our right. This was fitted with a McKenzie & Holland frame, and was recorded in 1921 as having eleven working levers with nine spare. It was abolished on 11th September 1949, and was subsequently demolished. The ELR station at Shoreditch is just about visible in the mist beyond the second overbridge. (British Rail)

31. Regular passenger traffic between Liverpool Street and the East London Line ceased from 31st March 1913, when the latter route was electrified, but the connection was retained until 17th April 1966 for goods traffic. It also proved very useful for through excursions linking stations on the GE system with destinations on the South Coast. Here we see one such train in the 1950s, having just passed over the junction behind a pair of ex-Great Eastern 0-6-0Ts. (B.P. Pask)

SPITALFIELDS

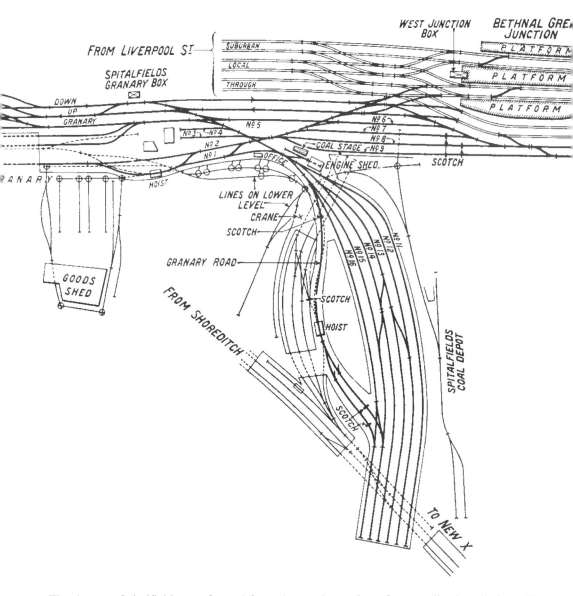

The depot at Spitalfields was formed from the amalgamation of two earlier installations. The first of these was known as Brick Lane, and was situated on the approach to the old Bishopsgate terminus, whilst the other, which was purely for coal traffic was located in Whitechapel. They were subsequently enlarged to form a single establishment, and became known as Spitalfields from 1st January 1881. In this diagram the Brick Lane goods shed is on the left, and the coal depot to the right. Below its southern tip runs the East London Railway, with a group of sidings branching to the north, which were connected to the depot by means of a wagon hoist. These ELR sidings occupied a formation originally intended as a through line connecting the East London and Great Eastern Railways between Bethnal Green Junction and Cambridge Heath, but although the civil engineering for this was well advanced by the second half of the 1860s, the scheme was abandoned. (Railway Magazine March 1933)

32.   Looking in a south-easterly direction from the street level section of Spitalfields depot, the electrified passenger tracks of the East London Line are seen on the right, with the non-electrified goods roads branching off to the left. The hydraulic lift which connected these to both tiers of the Great Eastern above was of sufficient length to take two wagons at a time, and had a capacity of 35 tons. This allowed exchange goods traffic to be operated between the two companies without having the inconvenience of reversing whole trains at Liverpool Street. Apart from this, the hoist was primarily used to lower wagons from the viaduct to street level, where the main depot facilities were located. (Stephenson Locomotive Society)

33.   Near the north end of the Spitalfields depot was a small engine shed. Standing beside this is Class C72 0-6-0T No. 24 as she pauses during shunting duties on 21st April 1914. (K.Nunn/LCGB)

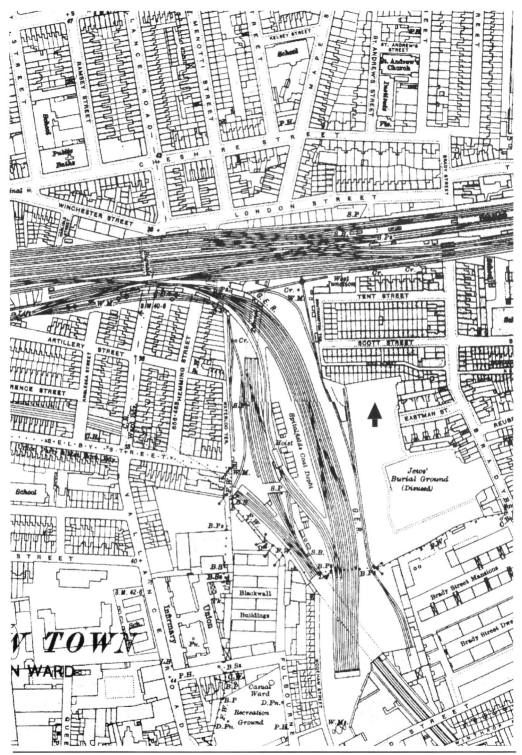

This OS map gives us a good impression of the area around Spitalfields depot in 1914. Traffic declined drastically in the 1960s and closure came on 6th November 1967. Bethnal Green station is centre right.

34. On 6th September 1953, The Railway Correspondence & Travel Society ran a special train to Cambridge, which departed from Bishopsgate goods station at 11.15am. Here it is seen passing Granary signal box behind Class D16/3 4-4-0 No. 62567. There had been a granary at Brick Lane depot since the late 1840s, and this gave its name to the box. Because of the amount of produce dealt with, it soon proved inadequate, so an adjoining warehouse was erected to its west. On 1st January 1919, these buildings caught fire, and because of their highly combustible contents, it was two days before they were extinguished. Granary signal box however, survived much longer and remained a feature until abolition on 9th October 1966. (K. Nunn/LCGB)

35.   At Bethnal Green West Junction, the line into Liverpool Street diverged from the original Bishopsgate route, and made a sharp descent towards the terminus. As part of this included a gradient of 1 in 65, it proved taxing for locomotives which were working services out of London. Here, large boilered Class T19 2-4-0 No. 760 climbs towards Bethnal Green, and passes Granary signal box seen on the high level lines to the left. (K. Nunn/LCGB)

BETHNAL GREEN

Bethnal Green opened on 24th May 1872 and replaced an earlier station to the east named Mile End. The reason for this being that Bethnal Green was to become the junction for a line to Hackney Downs and beyond, which was brought into use the same year. This OS map of 1872 shows us the layout with two side platforms and a central island. The commencement of the Spitalfields goods line can be seen at the bottom left hand corner, whilst the new route towards Hackney Downs diverges northward to the right.

36. From the window of a passing train we look west near Bethnal Green in the early 1960s, and catch a final glimpse of the siding complex which served Spitalfields depot. In the distance it is just possible to make out the shape of Granary signal box. (Norfolk Railway Society)

37. In this pre-grouping view of Bethnal Green Junction station, a train from Chingford heads towards Liverpool Street to the left, whilst the tracks for Bishopsgate diverge on the right. At the centre of the photograph stands Bethnal Green West Junction signal box, which dated from 1891, and was recorded thirty years later as having eighty-four working levers, together with six spare in its McKenzie & Holland frame. The structure at the end of the up main line suburban platform on the right which appears to be another signal box was in fact staffed by a timekeeper who advised signalmen along the route of any late running services which passed. The tall buildings with an impressive array of chimneypots to the left belong to an estate of model dwellings funded by Alderman Sydney Waterlow, and erected in the late 1860s. (British Rail)

38. Standing on the up main suburban platform in August 1909, we watch rebuilt Class T19 4-4-0 No. 719 passing with the 11-05am Liverpool Street-Hunstanton train. The platform faces used by services on the Hackney Downs group of lines lie behind the nameboard to the right. (K. Nunn/LCGB)

39. Standing with our backs to Waterlow Buildings in 1980, we look across Three Colts Lane to the corner of Tapp Street, where the station entrance was situated. This was in an architectural style much used by the GER in the 1870s, but sadly it has since been demolished. (J.E. Connor)

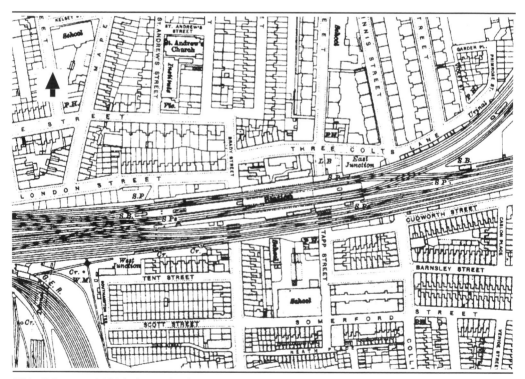

This OS map of 1914 shows the layout after the widening of 1891, with the new through lines passing south of the up main suburban platform, together with additional sidings accommodation for goods vehicles.

40.   Class B17/6 4-6-0 No. 1654 *Sunderland* blackening the sky as she approaches with a down express on 2nd December 1946. By this time Bethnal Green Junction West signal box was in its final days, as it was abolished from 13th April 1947, and subsequently removed. (H.C. Casserley)

41.   Under the New Works programme of the mid-1930s, Bethnal Green would have a station on the London Transport Central Line extension between Liverpool Street and Stratford. With this in place, it would be possible to transfer traffic from the existing LNER route, and therefore speed up services. Although work was delayed during World War ll, it was soon resumed after the end of hostilities, and the first section opened on 4th December 1946. LNER Stratford line services ceased to call at Bethnal Green from 8th December, and the up main suburban side together with one face of the island became redundant. This rather sad view of 2nd December 1946, looks eastwards along the soon to be closed platform. It has already lost its buildings, and the word 'Junction' has been deleted from the nameboard. The little stone drinking fountain on the island was a nice touch which survived into the late 1960s. (H.C. Casserley)

42.   Viewed from the island, Class B12/3 4-6-0 No. 61564 slowly passes with an up express on 7th July 1949. The site of the up main suburban platform was required for track alterations, so it was demolished immediately after closure. (R.A.P. Cogger/The Gresley Society)

43.   In November 1956, Class N7/3 0-6-2T No. 69685 approaching with a Hertford-Liverpool Street via Stratford train. The signal box to the left was brought into use in 1949, as part of the Shenfield Electrification scheme. (B.P. Pask)

44. The original buildings on the surviving platforms at Bethnal Green lasted into the 1980s, although the west end of their awnings were cut back around 1966. Looking towards Liverpool Street in 1975, the premises appear to be deserted, except that is for the lady on the right who has obviously seen something to interest her down in Three Colts Lane! (J.E. Connor)

45. A comprehensive re-signalling of the ex-GE main line meant that the distinctive boxes erected at the time of the Shenfield Electrification became redundant. Bethnal Green box is seen here from the window of a passing train. It closed in Spring 1989, and was demolished eight years later. (B.P. Pask)

GLOBE ROAD & DEVONSHIRE STREET

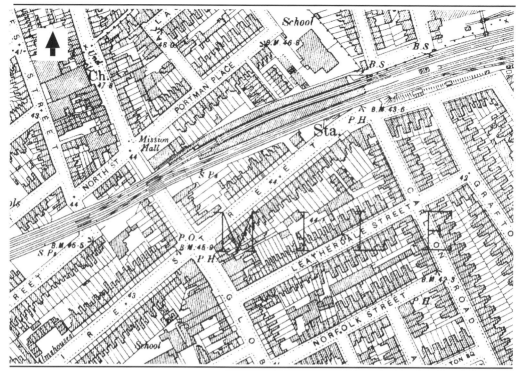

This station was constructed when the viaduct was being widened to take an additional pair of tracks for local traffic, and it opened on 1st July 1884. As can be seen from this OS map of ten years later, it had an entrance at its west end which faced onto Globe Road, and another to the east which served Devonshire Street. Both of these were located to the south of the formation, although the latter could also be accessed from Morpeth Street on the opposite side by means of a subway which led through the viaduct. Globe Road & Devonshire Street had platforms on the new local lines only, and until 1894 had a signal box which was located above the tracks at the London end. The station closed as a wartime economy measure on 22nd May 1916, and never reopened.

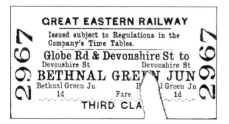

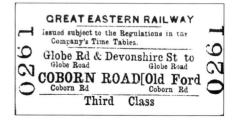

46. On entering the station, passengers passed through a pair of iron gates, then walked into the relevant booking hall, both of which were located within the arches of the viaduct. Here we see the entrance from Globe Road as it appeared in the 1950s, when part of the street level accommodation was being used by an engineering company. It had changed little since the time of closure, and until 1964 even retained a splendid cast-iron nameboard. The ornate scrolled ironwork beneath this formerly supported a pendant gaslamp. (H. Davies)

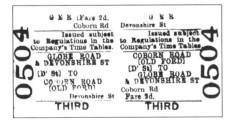

This artist's reconstruction is based on an engineer's drawing of May 1884 which shows one of the arches adapted as a station entrance. The surrounding brickwork was rendered in Portland cement, and stuccoed ornamentation was added to resemble rusticated stone. Both entrances were provided with canopies which displayed the station's name in gilded wooden letters, although the cramped siting of the Globe Road office probably meant that this was less visible than its counterpart at the other end.

47.   Taken in 1975, this view shows the arch which once accommodated the Devonshire Street booking office, and the changes which had taken place since closure. The glazed frontage and its attendant canopy had no doubt disappeared many years previously, but there was still ample remains of the Portland cement rendering. Perhaps the most surprising survival however, was the legend 'Great Eastern Railway' which was incised on the parapet, although this has since been removed. Devonshire Street itself is now known as Bancroft Road. (J.E. Connor)

48. Decent views of the station whilst still intact are extremely rare, and possibly non-existent, but we do have this rather sad photograph which was taken during demolition on 22nd March 1938. Looking from the London end, it can be seen that by then very little remained of the down platform. A bit more was still standing on the up side however, including one of the stairways and a section of rear wall. This had previously supported an awning of a similar style to that already seen at Bishopsgate Low Level and Bethnal Green, but as most of the rubble lying around appears to be brick it seems likely that this had been removed earlier. The signal box visible in the distance is Devonshire Street West. (British Rail)

G. E. R.

GLOBE ROAD AND
DEVONSHIRE ST.

49.　From a signal post at the country end of Globe Road station, we look east in June 1911 towards Devonshire Street West signal box. This was constructed during the widening of 1884 and replaced an earlier cabin to the south of the formation. The new local lines of 1884 are to the left of the box, whilst behind these, at a lower level, are the sidings of Devonshire Street goods yard, which opened in 1850. To the right of the picture are some additional sidings adjoining the main line, which were provided a few years later to serve coal drops. (British Rail)

PERISHABLE

From _____ *Chapel* DEVONSHIRE STREET

To _____ *Chapel*

Via _____

Consignee _____ *Turnall*

Truck No. _____

Owner & No. of Sheets }
　　& Under Sheets } _____

Date _____ 191

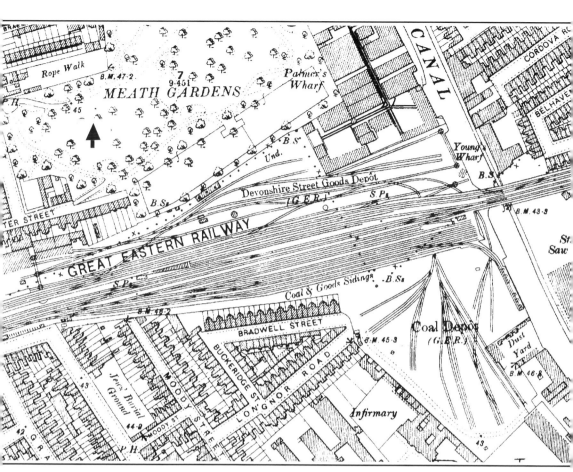

This OS map of 1894 shows the depot after it had been enlarged. The original section is to the north of the formation, whilst the slightly later coal drops are to the south. A decade or so before the widening of 1884, an incline was built north of the main line which descended in a westerly direction to serve additional sidings at street level. These were eventually connected to a new coal yard to the south by two sharply curving lines which passed beneath the viaduct, and terminated near the Regent's Canal. A further extension on this side prior to World War 1 gave additional vehicular access from Mile End Road, and from 1st September 1922, the depot was renamed Mile End & Devonshire Street.

G. E. R.
Globe Road

50. This is the main entrance to the 1850 yard, as seen about 1920. We are standing in a short section of road which paralleled the main line viaduct, and are looking over to the goods office which was located on the east side of Warley Street. The temporary Devonshire Street passenger terminus was located nearby, and although its exact siting is uncertain, there is a possibility it was served by a footpath off Prospect Place, which was swallowed up by the viaduct widening of 1884. (J.E. Connor Collection)

51. Because of the sharp curves encountered on the low level section, the GER were obliged to use short wheel-based locomotives to shunt the yard. Here, Class 209 0-4-0ST No 227 is seen on 19th April 1909, as she stands beside the wooden Devonshire Street coaling stage. (K. Nunn/LCGB)

52. Another renaming took place on 1st January 1939, when the depot became known as Mile End, and all reference to Devonshire Street was dropped. This nameboard, photographed in 1975, faced onto Bancroft Road, and was displayed near the site of the former eastern entrance to Globe Road passenger station. (J.E. Connor)

53. Looking west along the low level yard in the early 1960s, the overhead wires and girder bridge of the main line are seen to our left. The northern part of the depot handled perishable goods and general merchandise, although latterly the principal traffic was coal. Mile End was officially closed from 6th November 1967, but sand and ballast trains continued to use the sidings to the south. (Norfolk Railway Society)

54. Mile End signal box was located south of the main line, and adjoined the west bank of the Regents Canal. It was built as part of the Shenfield Electrification scheme, and replaced Devonshire Street East box which was abolished on 6th February 1949. Like Bethnal Green seen earlier it was rendered redundant by a later resignalling scheme, and was demolished on Saturday 20th April 1996. (J.E. Connor)

COBORN ROAD (OLD FORD) 1st STATION

This station was opened on 1st February 1865, and was located to the east of Coborn Road. It was originally named Old Ford, and consisted of two platforms, with buildings at the London end. As can be seen from the OS map of 1870, the immediate surroundings remained largely undeveloped at the time, although a few houses were beginning to appear. From 1st March 1879 the station was renamed Coborn Road (Old Ford), and it remained in use until 2nd December 1883, when it was resited in connection with the widening which was then under way.

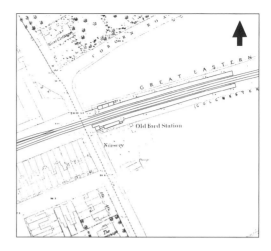

GREAT EASTERN RAILWAY.

OLD FORD STATION.

Trains, calling at Old Ford, leave the Bishopsgate Station at

7 20 a.m.	12 15 p.m.	4 15 p.m.	7 22 p.m.
9 7 ,,	1 15 ,,	5 22 ,,	8 22 ,,
10 15 ,,	2 15 ,,	6 22 ,,	9 22 ,,
11 15 ,,	3 15 ,,	6 35 ,,	10 22 ,,

Trains to Bishopsgate leave Old Ford at

7 51 a.m.	9 41 a.m.	2 45 p.m.	7 42 p.m.
8 16 ,,	10 35 ,,	3 41 ,,	8 45 ,,
8 45 ,,	11 45 ,,	4 45 ,,	9 38 ,,
9 2 ,,	12 45 p.m.	5 45 ,,	
9 24 ,,	1 45 ,,	6 40 ,,	

FARES BETWEEN BISHOPSGATE AND OLD FORD:

	SINGLE.	RETURN.
First Class -	4d.	6d.
Second Class	3d.	4d.

Superintendent's Office,
London, May, 1866.

BY ORDER.

PRINTED AT THE COMPANY'S WORKS, STRATFORD.

COBORN ROAD (OLD FORD) 2nd STATION

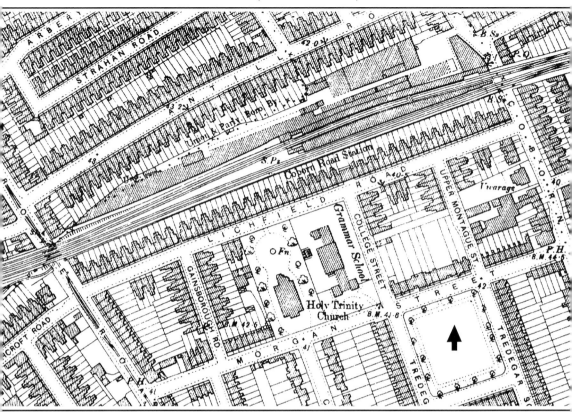

The second Coborn Road (Old Ford) station, which was opened on 2nd December 1883, stood to the west of its predecessor, and occupied a site previously used by a pair of sidings. It was brought into use before the widening had been completed, by slewing the running lines to the north so that they passed through the new platforms. Apart from this, the widening of the stretch between James Street (near Globe Road) and Bow Junction was carried out by constructing an additional track either side of the existing formation.

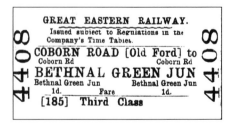

55. The second station at Coborn Road had two entrances, of which the westernmost served Grove Road. This view looks south along that thoroughfare in the early twentieth century, and the gates are just visible adjoining the bridge abutment on the left hand side. Although far from clear, they appear to be of a similar style to those already encountered at Globe Road & Devonshire Street. Once through these gates, passengers walked along a footpath which followed the railway, and eventually reached the entrance proper. The booking hall at this end was referred to as the 'Grove Road Office' and was denoted on tickets by the initials 'GRO'. (Lens of Sutton)

56. A northward view features Coborn Road itself. The station entrance was on the left hand side beyond the bridge, but is unfortunately not visible. (Lens of Sutton)

57. An up suburban train is seen arriving in the early twentieth century. Coborn Road signal box was built on a gantry above the tracks, and was brought into use in 1884. (Lens of Sutton)

Like Bishopsgate Low Level and Globe Road, the station was closed as a wartime economy measure on 22nd May 1916, although there was a great deal of local protest. According to a contemporary newspaper report *"a number of passengers presented themselves on Monday morning at the booking office, to see if the threat of the company had actually been carried out. They found the doors closed, and later in the day men appeared and boarded up the windows also. On Tuesday preparations were made for painting out the large notices on the iron bridge "Frequent trains to the City."...The name of the station is pasted over with a placard reading Station Closed."*

58. Unlike Bishopsgate and Globe Road, Coborn Road reopened after hostilities had ended, and was brought back to use on 5th May 1919. In this view, taken from the west end, part of the Grove Road Office frontage is visible to the left. The station only served the local lines, and no platforms were ever provided on the through tracks seen to the right. (British Rail)

59. The station was to be closed under the Shenfield Electrification scheme, but the onset of World War ll delayed this from taking place, although the awnings were subsequently shortened. Here we are looking from the Grove Road end on 3rd June 1942, and judging by the lack of activity it seems as if the demolition men have disappeared into the cafe across the road for their tea break! (British Rail)

60. Moving eastwards, similar demolition work was also in progress at this end. Life appears to be carrying on as normal, although a barrage balloon in the sky reminds us of the ever-present threat of air-raids. (British Rail)

61. By 20th August 1942, the awnings had been shortened, and the station was in the process of being tidied up. This view is from the west end, and a section of the Grove Road Office entrance can just be seen near the bottom left hand corner. (British Rail)

62. In the small hours of 13th June 1944, East End firewatchers saw what they thought to be an enemy plane flying low over the rooftops unperturbed by search-lights and anti-aircraft barrage. It sounded very different to the usual raiders, and appeared to have a light coming from its tail. Once over Bow however, it suddenly stopped and fell from the sky. Rumours soon spread that it was an experimental plane being tried by the Luftwaffe, and the pilot had been captured in Aldgate after baling out. In fact it was the first of Hitler's V1 flying bombs, or 'doodlebugs' as they became known, and it had made a direct hit on the bridge over Grove Road. Despite the dreadful damage, engineers were soon on site, and within thirty-six hours they had erected a temporary bridge so that two of the four roads into Liverpool Street could be reopened. Here a Class N7 0-6-2T approaches gingerly with what appears to be a Liverpool Street-Stratford empty stock working on 14th June. The bridge now carries a British Heritage commemorative plaque. (British Rail)

63. After the war, the station's days were clearly numbered. Looking west towards the signal box and surviving sections of canopy, it can be seen that the stairways which once served the Grove Road entrance have been demolished. (H.C. Casserley)

64. From the London end of the station, Class B17/6 4-6-0 No. 1620 *Clumber* rattles through tender first with a down empty stock train on 2nd December 1946. It appears as if the name-board has been temporarily fixed to the part-demolished rear wall, and has lost the first 'O' from its name in the process. (H.C. Casserley)

65. This view looks east from beneath the surviving section of up side awning towards the stairways on the same day. The rear wall which would have been to the right has been replaced by a temporary fence, but that on the other side remains intact. (H.C. Casserley)

66. Towards the end, the partially demolished station looked very forlorn indeed. Here a down train passes through behind Class F6 2-4-2T No. 7238 on 2nd December 1946, just six days before permanent closure. The extension of the LPTB Central Line from Liverpool Street to Stratford was due to open on 4th December, and as this would parallel the existing route, regular Coborn Road passengers were advised to use the nearby Underground station at Mile End instead. (H.C. Casserley)

67. A final look at Coborn Road with this view of Class N7/4 0-6-2T No. 9614 pausing with an Ilford-Liverpool Street via Fairlop Loop train. The station closed after Sunday 8th December 1946, following the departure of the 1.20am service from Liverpool Street to Brentwood. After this, the demolition was so rapid that by May of the following year the up side had virtually disappeared. The signal box was abolished from 6th February 1949, and was subsequently removed. All that remained of the station in 1999 were the remnants of the down platform, together with a section of rear wall, and its derelict stairway. (H.C. Casserley)

BOW JUNCTION

In 1845, a line was authorised to connect the London & Blackwall Railway at Stepney with the Eastern Counties Railway near Bow. However, three years later, whilst construction was under way, the ECR refused to sanction a physical junction between the two routes supposedly because they felt it might lead to accidents. A temporary connection was laid in December 1848 to allow the passage of some new locomotives for the L&BR, but was then lifted. The line opened for traffic on 2nd April 1849, but it ended at stop-blocks near the intended junction, where an interchange station known as Victoria Park & Bow was erected.

There was a long-running dispute between the two companies, and the station was never used to its full potential. The ECR refused to issue through tickets to Fenchurch Street and provided the new premises with an extremely poor service, therefore completely reducing its value as an interchange. After much wrangling, the situation improved, but traffic never really developed, and when the East & West India Docks & Birmingham Junction Railway (later North London Railway) began running a service between Fenchurch Street and their own station at Bow in 1850, the L&BR trains were withdrawn.

The ECR continued using their side of Victoria Park & Bow for a little longer, but ceased doing so from 6th January 1851, when the station was officially closed.

Changes on the ECR Board of Directors, and the advent of the London Tilbury & Southend Railway eventually brought a thaw in the relationship between the the companies, and the junction was finally laid in 1854.

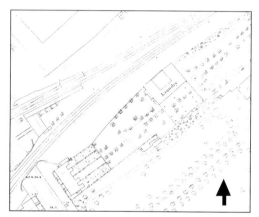

Near the top left hand corner of this OS map of 1867, we can see what appears to be the disused ECR platforms at Victoria Park & Bow station, together with the former street level entrance in Fairfield Road. By this time however, all trace of the L&BR side seems to have disappeared.

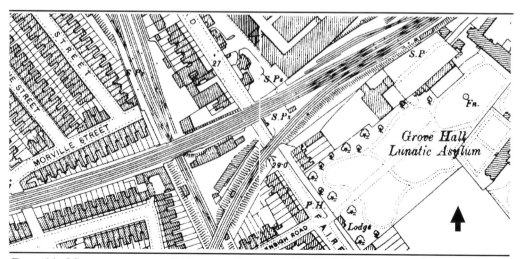

From this OS map, we can see the layout as it appeared in 1893. The line to the left which passes beneath the Great Eastern and Blackwall Extension Railways is the North London Poplar branch.

68. This view looks west towards Bow Junction, and shows the signal box in the middle distance. This dated from 1893, and replaced an earlier box to the north of the formation which was removed to provide space for a new up local line. The box was badly damaged by bombing during World War ll, but repaired, and not closed until 24th July 1949, when it was replaced as part of the Shenfield Electrification scheme. (British Rail)

69. Bow Junction is seen here from a passing train in the early 1990s. On the extreme left is the Docklands Light Railway, followed by the connection to Fenchurch Street, singled in the previous decade, but retained for empty stock movements. Next comes the 1949 signal box, which was demolished in the Spring of 1996, and finally the Great Eastern main line. (J.E. Connor)

STRATFORD

Our route runs diagonally across the page. A station was opened at Stratford by the Eastern Counties Railway on 20th June 1839, and provided with two platforms. These were later joined by an additional pair which were constructed for the Northern & Eastern Railway. At first both sets of premises were separate from each other, but from 1st April 1847, they were combined to make one single station. The OS map shown here dates from 1893, and provides us with an idea of just how complex the network of lines had become by then. Near the bottom left is Stratford Western Junction, where the Carpenters Curve branched off in a north-westerly direction towards Channelsea

Junction and Victoria Park. A little further along, the Stratford Southern Curve can be seen diverging in the opposite direction, and eventually leading to the North Woolwich line. Continuing northwards, past Central Junction, is the station, with the old N&ER tracks curving north, and the main line continuing straight ahead. The nearby signal box is Stratford Central. The Low Level platforms, serving the North Woolwich branch, can be seen immediately south of the main line, whilst above, between the Victoria Park branch and the Northern & Eastern line lies the vast expanse of Stratford Works and locomotive depot.

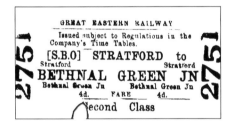

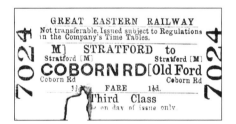

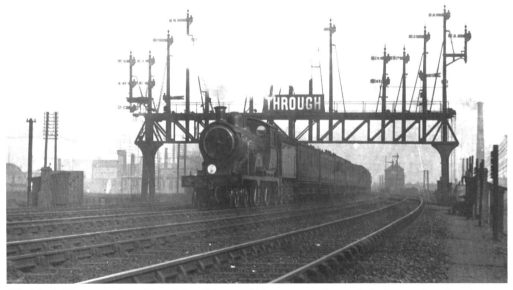

70. The 9.02am train from Norwich to Liverpool Street passes beneath the impressive signal gantry at Stratford Western Junction on 6th March 1913, behind Class S46 4-4-0 No. 1880. The signal gantry stretching above six tracks was erected in 1892, and carried the word 'Through' in stencilled letters above the fast lines. (K. Nunn/LCGB)

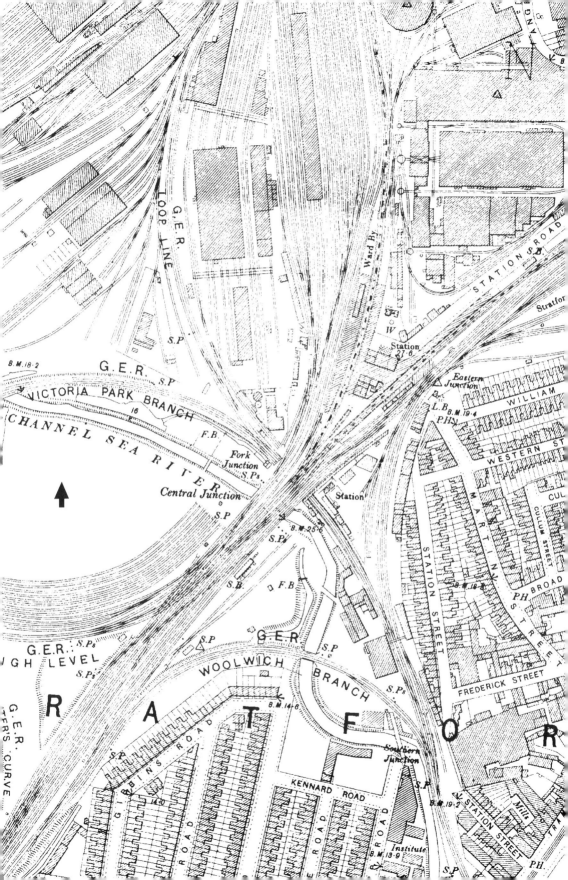

71. A group of passengers on the down local platform await the arrival of an incoming train in the early twentieth century. The station had been reconstructed at various times since opening, and on one of these occasions, in 1898, the up local platform, which is seen to the left, was altered to an island so that it could also serve the down through line. (Lens of Sutton)

72. With the island now on the right, we look again towards Liverpool Street, and just about see the Martin Street entrance behind the small buildings near the centre of the picture. The staggered platform in the middle distance was built at the London end in 1900, and served a new up loop line. The wagons on the left are standing in the goods depot yard. (British Rail)

73. The Martin Street entrance to the station, as it appeared in the 1930s. It was opened in 1886, and was similar in styling to other GER street level buildings of its period, particularly Bow Road on the line between Stratford and Fenchurch Street. It remained largely in its original condition for many years, although one of the windows was latterly altered to accommodate a tobacconists shop. To the right is the passageway entrance which led to the works and locomotive depot, whilst above this stand the main line platforms. (British Rail)

74. This view from the up loop platform looks north across to the main part of the station in the 1930s, with the former Northern & Eastern Railway route curving off to the left, and the main line to Ilford on the right. (J.E. Connor collection)

75. A Class S69 4-6-0 blows off on the up local side as she awaits the road in 1922. Behind her we see the additional platform, which was opened in 1900, and accommodated Stratford Central signal box near its London end. The former Northern & Eastern Railway route towards Lea Bridge and Tottenham curves off on the right. (British Rail)

76. Class N7/2 0-6-2T No. 2639 stands at the up local platform in the 1930s with an Ilford-Liverpool Street train. To the right is the stairway which led from the Martin Street entrance to the up platform of 1900. (J.E. Connor collection)

77. Class N2/1 0-6-2T No. 4740 awaiting departure with a Shenfield line train in the 1930s. A few N2s worked on the Great Eastern Section during this period, but most were transferred back to their native Great Northern territory between 1938 and 1940. (Photomatic)

78. Under the 1930s electrification scheme, the Shenfield and Central Line trains were to be accommodated at new platforms to the south of the formation. Work on these was well in hand by 1940, but was delayed by the intensification of enemy activity, and not completed until after World War ll had ended. In this view from 30th June 1948, we see Class F5 2-4-2T No. 67203 arriving at the newly completed Platform 8 with a Liverpool Street-Ilford train, a little over a year before the electric service was inaugurated. (H.C. Casserley)

79. One of the new electric trains departs for Liverpool Street from platform 5 on 1st October 1949. To the left, the former Stratford Central signal box, which had been abolished on 4th September 1949, is being demolished. To the right, but not quite visible is Platform 4, which was one of the bays intended for the aborted electric shuttle service to and from Fenchurch Street. (D.B. Slaughter)

80. The Central Line tracks were brought to surface level by steeply graded inclines at either end of the station. Here a train of Standard Tube Stock climbs towards Platform 3 on its journey to Ealing Broadway in the 1950s. To the extreme right can be seen the rear of the new entrance completed on 6th October 1946 to replace the Martin Street building of 1886. (J.E. Connor Collection)

81. With the Shenfield electrification, the lines to the south of the formation were designated for local traffic, whilst fast trains used those to the north. The existing platforms on this side were retained, although the old island had to be altered to suit the new layout, and became Platform 9. Here an up express is seen taking the through road between Platforms 8 and 9 behind Class 7 4-6-2 No. 70008 *Black Prince* in the 1950s. (Photomatic)

82. Still on the main line side, Class B17/1 4-6-0 No. 61625 *Raby Castle* passes through on 6th August 1956. (R.A. Panting)

83. A view from the London end of Platform 8 in July 1958, as Class B12/3 4-6-0 No. 61577 hurries past on the through lines with a down express. (B.P. Pask)

84. From the same vantage point we see Class B1 4-6-0 No. 61027 *Madoqua* in immaculate BR lined black livery bringing a freight off the curve from Channelsea Junction during July 1959. (B.P. Pask)

85. From the London end of Platform 9, the view is across to No 10 in 1965. The canopy on this was rationalised soon after, and has since been replaced by one of much shorter length. The building on No 9 survived until early 1994, when it was demolished to facilitate platform rebuilding. (J.E. Connor)

86. A new subway approach to the 1946 station entrance in the 1970s brought various external changes, although the building still survived at the beginning of 1999. Here it is seen with its once illuminated awning still in position, whilst preparatory work for the subway was in its early stages. (J.E. Connor)

87. With the advent of the Docklands Light Railway, a use was at last found for Platform 4, one of the bays which had been constructed for the Fenchurch Street shuttles and never used. Class P86 vehicle No 01 is shown here on a trial run in July 1987, a month prior to the line's public opening. The westbound Central Line track descends to the right. (J.E. Connor)

88. In addition to that in Martin Street, a larger, more imposing entrance was located at the south-western end of Station Road, and emerged between what are now Platforms 10 and 11. It was conveniently sited for the area known as 'New Town' but was latterly little used and therefore closed from 23rd October 1944. Since then the building became increasingly derelict, although the shell remained standing in 1999. (I. Baker)

89. The first section of Stratford Works opened in 1847, and over the years it grew into a huge complex. Many locomotives were built here including such famous classes as the *Claud Hamilton* 4-4-0s, and the original B12 4-6-0s. The last new engine to emerge from the erecting shop was Class N7 0-6-2T No 999E which entered traffic in March 1924, and is now preserved at the East Anglian Railway Museum, Chappel & Wakes Colne. In this view, we are in the section known as The Old Works as No 69668, one of 999E's later classmates, undergoes an overhaul on 15th January 1961. As can be seen, there was little activity towards the end of steam, but although the works closed in September 1963, more modern forms of traction continued to be repaired elsewhere at Stratford until March 1991. (K.C.H. Fairey)

90. At one time, Stratford boasted the largest locomotive depot in the country. Class J69/1 0-6-0T No 358E and Class N7 0-6-2T No 8001 are posed nicely in the shed yard soon after the grouping. In the background is a part of a huge coaling plant, which was brought into use in 1922, and demolished early in 1963. (Lens of Sutton)

MARYLAND

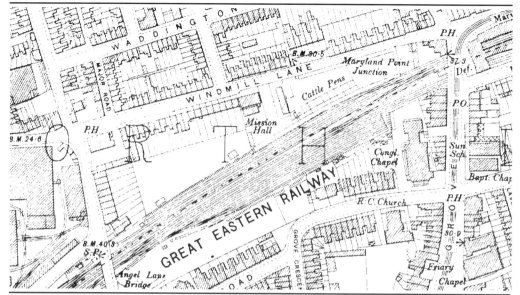

Opened as Maryland Point on 6th January 1873, the station was completely rebuilt in 1891-2 when the track was quadrupled. This OS map from 1894 shows the layout as it was at that time, with platforms on the slow lines only, and an entrance at each end.

91.   The main street level building was located at the junction of The Grove and Maryland Point, and was entered through a doorway near its north-western corner. This view dates from 16th July 1936, and shows the frontage after a few superficial alterations had been made. The name of the hairdresser with the uncompromisingly art-deco facade to our right was pronounced locally as *"Mason 'Enry"*. (British Rail)

92. The entrance at the east end was smaller than its western counterpart, and faced onto Water Lane. This view shows its frontage in the 1930s, and also the large Presbyterian Church located near the junction of Maryland Point and Leytonstone Road. (British Rail)

93. The electrification scheme involved the two pairs of tracks changing roles, therefore those to the north of the formation became the through lines, and those to the south took local traffic. This view, which dates from 19th June 1940, is looking down from the Water Lane booking hall and shows the various alterations which were then taking place. The up platform has been stripped of buildings, and is being prepared for conversion into an island, whilst the length of the down side awning has been cut back to allow space for a new street level building. (British Rail)

94. The station was renamed Maryland on 28th October 1940, but very little else was done until the end of World War ll. Looking east along the down platform in the second half of the 1940s, it can be seen that the work had well and truly recommenced. The metal framework for both the new street level building and the island platform canopy was in position, and it looks as if progress was also being made on the additional platform on the south side. (Lens of Sutton)

95. This is the new street level building as it appeared in the 1970s. It stands on the south side of Maryland Point, and replaced the two earlier entrances. That at Water Lane disappeared completely, but a fragment of the other survived, and could still be seen in 1999. (J.E. Connor)

96.   Although built in the 1940s, the style of the platform buildings at Maryland betrayed their pre-war origins. With their cream and blue tiling, and sweeping curved ends, they belonged very much to the 1930s. Viewed from a similar position to that chosen by the photographer in Picture No 94, we look towards the island. After rebuilding, only the platform faces on the slow lines were officially used, although access to the side serving the down main was retained in case it was required in an emergency, or during engineering works. (J.E. Connor)

97.   The last of the 1949 Electrics, latterly known as Class 306, was taken out of public service towards the end of 1981, but unit No 017 was retained and restored into green livery at Ilford Depot. Since 1986 it has been used on various special workings, and it is seen here on one such occasion, as it heads through Maryland en-route to Liverpool Street. Although the station still retains many of its 1940s features, the distinctive platform buildings with their rounded ends have been removed. (J.E. Connor)

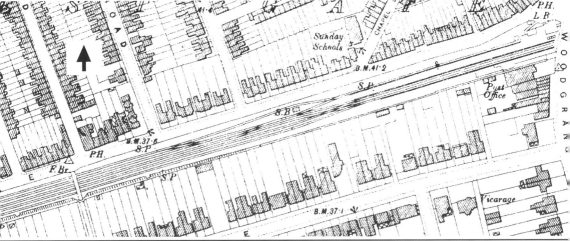

The station opened in 1840, but as the area was still undeveloped, traffic was extremely light, so it was closed from 1st June 1843. Following protests from the scant local population, it was reopened on 31st May 1846, although there was little demand for it until the advent of urbanisation about two decades later. The old station comprised two 350ft platforms, and had its entrance on the down side in Forest Lane. As more people moved into the district, this eventually proved to be inadequate, so a rebuilding scheme was implemented, and completed by 1st June 1870, when a new entrance was provided from Woodgrange Road. Two years later, the platforms were lengthened by an additional 100ft, and a bay was provided for terminating trains on the down side. The OS map of 1894 shows the station immediately prior to quadrupling, before work had started on its comprehensive rebuilding.

98. Looking north along Woodgrange Road in the first decade of the twentieth century we have the street level building on the left, which was constructed at the time of the quadrupling. This was positioned above the tracks, whereas its predecessor of 1870 stood to the north of them. In this view, West Ham Corporation tramcar No 16 rattles by. The tramways of this area are featured in the Middleton Press albums *East Ham & West Ham Tramways* and *Ilford & Barking Tramways*. (Lens of Sutton)

99. As with Maryland Point, platforms were only provided on the local lines. This eastward view from 16th July 1936 features the footbridge which served a supplementary entrance from Forest Road. This closed in 1940, when rebuilding was under way, and was never reinstated. (British Rail)

100. From the bottom of the stairs leading from the Forest Road entrance, we have a view along the down platform towards the main street level building in Woodgrange Road. Judging from earlier photographs it appears that the rather unusual arrangement of two separate sets of awnings on each side dated from the rebuilding of 1894-5. (British Rail)

101. We have now moved into the post World War ll era, and see the 1890s station very much in its last days. The up side buildings have been removed so that the platform can be rebuilt as an island, and builders materials are much in evidence. The nameboard visible near the centre of the picture includes the suffix 'For Upton', which was not perpetuated after rebuilding. (Lens of Sutton)

102. Standing at the west end of the island in the 1950s, we look towards the new up platform which was completed in the previous decade. The earlier down side, which is just visible to the left, was retained for possible use during emergencies, but was stripped of its buildings. (Norfolk Railway Society)

FOREST GATE JUNCTION

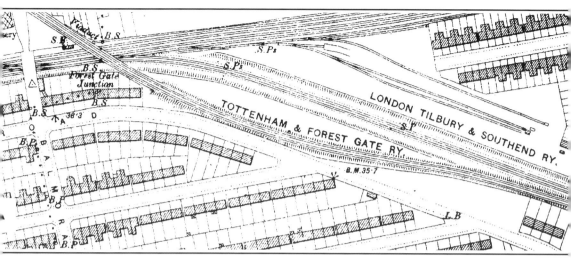

This 1894 OS map feature Forest Gate Junction, where the original London Tilbury & Southend Railway route of 1854 diverged from the Eastern Counties main line. The Tottenham & Forest Gate Joint Railway was a later addition, which opened in 1894, and now forms part of the present Barking-Gospel Oak route. The sidings which are shown alongside the LTSR tracks served Forest Gate goods depot, which closed on 7th December 1970.

103. The final Forest Gate Junction signal box was located on the down side, immediately west of the bridge carrying the Barking-Gospel Oak line. A major resignalling scheme resulted in its closure on 26th August 1996, and it was demolished in December of the same year. (B.P. Pask)

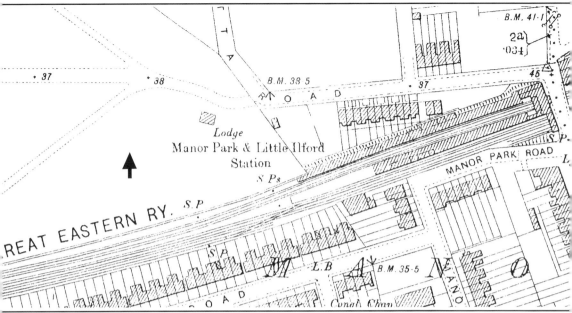

Manor Park station opened on 6th January 1873, and comprised two platforms. It was completely rebuilt in connection with the quadrupling of 1894, and provided with a new street level building at its east end. This OS map shows the layout soon after rebuilding.

104.   This is the 1894 street level building, as it appeared in the early twentieth century. It was damaged by enemy action on 24th July 1944, and although patched up afterwards, it was never quite the same again. (J.E. Connor collection)

105. In this post World War ll view we are looking east, and see that both sides still retained structures which dated from the quadrupling of 1894. Scars from the bombing incident of 1944 are noticeable at the far end, particularly with regard to the street level building, which has lost part of its roof. The nameboard to the right bears traces of the suffix 'Little Ilford', which the company originally intended as the station's title, but changed it to Manor Park before opening. (Lens of Sutton)

106. The rebuilt station was similar in styling to those at Maryland and Forest Gate, and included the distinctive platform buildings with curved ends. Here we are again looking east, but this time we are standing on the island. The new up local platform built in the 1940s is on the right, whilst the earlier down side, which is no longer in regular use, can be seen on the extreme left. (J.E. Connor)

ILFORD

107.   This view dates from around 1890, and shows the station when it comprised just two platforms. We are looking east from the down side, towards the main building, which is thought to have been constructed for the opening on 20th June 1839. The lofty shelter to the right had previously covered a siding, and may have been used for carriage storage. The stretch of platform in front of this was dangerously narrow, so the siding was lifted in 1886, and the platform widened over its former site. The footbridge seen to the left was erected in 1881, whilst the down side building, behind it, was added during the following year. (London Borough of Redbridge Libraries)

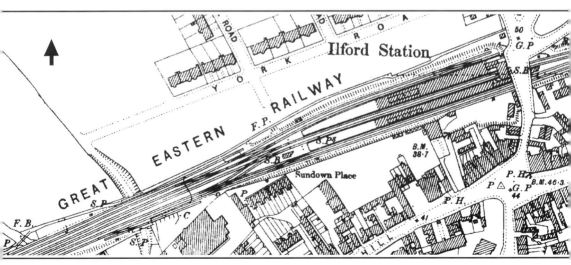

Like the other stations on the line, Ilford was rebuilt at the time of quadrupling, although until 1st July 1898, platforms were provided on the local lines only. This extract from an OS map dates from 1894, and shows the layout before these and an entrance at the western end were added.

108. The main entrance was that which faced onto Cranbrook Road, and dated from the time of rebuilding. In 1895 however, additional access was provided from York Road, and comprised a small street level building connected to the station's western end by means of a footbridge. Here this secondary entrance can be seen in the 1980s. (B.P. Pask)

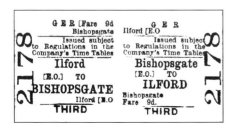

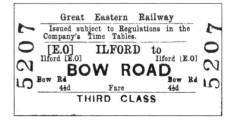

109. From beneath the York Road footbridge, we look along the through lines towards the main entrance in Cranbrook Road in GER days. The building in the centre originally had a blank wall on this side, and had to be provided with doors and windows when its platform was converted into an island in 1898. (Lens of Sutton)

110. Looking in the opposite direction, we enjoy the spectacle of seeing one of only two streamlined locomotives ever to work regularly on ex-GER metals. She was Class B17/5 4-6-0 No. 2870 *City of London*, and she was outshopped in this manner during 1937 to work the *East Anglian* express from London to Norwich. Here she appears to be on a less glamourous duty, and is passing Ilford West signal box. The ominous presence of sandbags on the platform tell us that the date is probably 1939. (Lens of Sutton)

111. No drastic alterations were made to the station in connection with the Shenfield Electrification scheme, but a flyover was constructed to the west at Aldersbrook. This carried the slow lines from south of the formation over to the north, so that they could regain their original position through Ilford station and beyond. Work on the flyover was well advanced by 1940, but with the intervention of war, its opening was delayed until 6th October 1947. This view dates from 1950. (British Rail)

112. Class B17/6 4-6-0 No. 61668 *Bradford City* comes off the Aldersbrook flyover and approaches the station on a special working in July 1958. The signal box on the left, replaced the last of the earlier Ilford boxes in 1949, and remained in use until 26th August 1996. (B.P. Pask)

113. Standing on the up through platform, we have Class B1 4-6-0 No. 61311 beneath the York Road footbridge with a football excursion train in the 1950s. (B.P. Pask)

114. Another excursion train is seen at the up through platform, but this time it is headed by Class N7 0-6-2T No. 69719 in July 1958. (B.P. Pask)

115. Still in the 1950s, we look eastwards along the local lines. The bridge in the foreground was erected in 1911 for the conveyance of milkchurns, and linked all platforms. At that time, a great number of churns were being handled at Ilford, so lifts were provided to ease the burden of platform staff who had to carry them. Milk traffic was eventually lost to road competition, but the bridge was retained for parcels use until its removal in the 1980s. The same decade also saw the awning on the up through platform being drastically reduced in length. (Norfolk Railway Society)

116. As part of the 1893 rebuilding, a bay platform was provided on the down side, and this is shown in 1968. New stairways were provided in 1925 when alterations were made in the booking hall, and one of these is visible on the left. The station canopies lost their distinctive 1890s valencing in 1985, although the replacement roofing utilised the original ironwork. (J.E. Connor)

117. Looking towards Liverpool Street in 1972, with one of the Class 306 units passing beneath the York Road footbridge. (J.E. Connor)

118. In 1978 the York Road footbridge was rebuilt, and placed slightly higher in connection with alterations to the overhead wiring. Here we see it as EMU No 309 626, festooned with balloons, passes underneath the bridge whilst working a children's' excursion organised by the staff at Ilford Car Sheds. (B.P. Pask)

119. Although access to the station from York Road was still available in 1999, the booking office was closed in 1991, and replaced by a ticket machine. Here we look inside and see the fine LNER passimeter around the time of closure. These offices were once commonplace throughout suburban London, but this was the last to remain in use. (B.P. Pask)

120. The main street level building was partially rebuilt in the 1960s, but remained standing until the mid-1980s, when complete demolition took place. A new entrance was then erected on the same site,and we finish our journey by looking at this, having covered 7 miles 27 chains, and 160 years since starting out. (B.P. Pask)

MP Middleton Press
EVOLVING THE ULTIMATE RAIL ENCYCLOPEDIA
Easebourne Lane, Midhurst, West Sussex.
GU29 9AZ Tel:01730 813169
www.middletonpress.co.uk email:info@middletonpress.co.uk
A-0 906520 B-1 873793 C-1 901706 D-1 904474

A
Abergavenny to Merthyr C 91 5
Abertillery and Ebbw Vale Lines D 84 5
Aldgate & Stepney Tramways B 70 7
Allhallows - Branch Line to A 62 2
Alton - Branch Lines to A 11 8
Andover to Southampton A 82 7
Ascot - Branch Lines around A 64 9
Ashburton - Branch Line to B 95 2
Ashford - Steam to Eurostar B 67 7
Ashford to Dover A 48 7
Austrian Narrow Gauge D 04 7
Avonmouth - BL around D 42 X
B
Banbury to Birmingham D 27 6
Barking to Southend C 80 X
Barnet & Finchley Tramways B 93 6
Barry - Branch Lines around D 50 0
Basingstoke to Salisbury A 89 4
Bath Green Park to Bristol C 36 2
Bath to Evercreech Junction A 60 6
Bath Tramways B 86 3
Battle over Portsmouth 1940 A 29 0
Battle over Sussex 1940 A 79 7
Bedford to Wellingborough D 31 4
Betwixt Petersfield & Midhurst A 94 0
Blitz over Sussex 1941-42 B 35 9
Bodmin - Branch Lines around B 83 9
Bognor at War 1939-45 B 59 6
Bombers over Sussex 1943-45 B 51 0
Bournemouth & Poole Trys B 47 2
Bournemouth to Evercreech Jn A 46 0
Bournemouth to Weymouth A 57 6
Bournemouth Trolleybuses C 10 9
Bradford Trolleybuses D 19 5
Brecon to Neath D 43 8
Brecon to Newport D 16 0
Brickmaking in Sussex B 19 7
Brightons Tramways B 02 2 OOP
Brighton to Eastbourne A 16 9
Brighton to Worthing A 03 7
Brighton Trolleybuses D 34 9
Bristols Tramways B 57 X
Bristol to Taunton D 03 9
Bromley South to Rochester B 23 5
Bromsgrove to Gloucester D 73 X
Brunel - A railtour of his achievements D 74 8
Bude - Branch Line to B 29 4
Burnham to Evercreech Jn A 68 1
Burton & Ashby Tramways C 51 6
C
Camberwell & West Norwood Tys B 22 7
Cambridge to Ely D 55 1
Canterbury - Branch Lines around B 58 8
Cardiff Trolleybuses D 64 0
Caterham & Tattenham Corner B 25 1
Changing Midhurst C 15 X
Chard and Yeovil - BLs around C 30 3
Charing Cross to Dartford A 75 4
Charing Cross to Orpington A 96 7
Cheddar - Branch Line to B 90 1
Cheltenham to Andover C 43 5
Cheltenham to Redditch D 81 0
Chesterfield Tramways D 37 3
Chesterfield Trolleybuses D 51 9
Chichester to Portsmouth A 14 2
Clapham & Streatham Trys B 97 9 OOP
Clapham Junction - 50 yrs C 06 0 OOP
Clapham Junction to Beckenham Jn B 36 7
Clevedon & Portishead - BLs to D 18 7
Collectors Trains, Trolleys & Trams D 29 2
Colonel Stephens D62 4
Cornwall Narrow Gauge D 56 X
Crawley to Littlehampton A 34 7
Cromer - Branch Lines around C 26 5
Croydons Tramways B 42 1
Croydons Trolleybuses B 73 1 OOP
Croydon to East Grinstead B 48 0
Crystal Palace (HL) & Catford Loop A 87 8
D
Darlington Trolleybuses D 33 0
Dartford to Sittingbourne B 34 0
Derby Tramways D 17 9
Derby Trolleybuses C 72 9
Derwent Valley - Branch Line to the D 06 3
Didcot to Banbury D 02 0
Didcot to Swindon C 84 2
Didcot to Winchester C 13 3
Dorset & Somerset Narrow Gauge D 76 4
Douglas to Peel C 88 5
Douglas to Port Erin C 55 9
Douglas to Ramsey D 39 X
Dovers Tramways B 24 3
Dover to Ramsgate A 78 9
E
Ealing to Slough C 42 7
Eastbourne to Hastings A 27 4 OOP
East Cornwall Mineral Railways D 22 5
East Croydon to Three Bridges A 53 3
East Grinstead - Branch Lines to A 07 X
East Ham & West Ham Tramways B 52 9
East Kent Light Railway A 61 4 OOP
East London - Branch Lines of C 44 3
East London Line B 80 4
East Ridings Secret Resistance D 21 7
Edgware & Willesden Tramways C 18 4
Effingham Junction - BLs around A 74 6
Eltham & Woolwich Tramways B 74 X OOP
Ely to Kings Lynn C 53 2
Ely to Norwich C 90 7
Embankment & Waterloo Tramways B 41 3
Enfield & Wood Green Trys C 03 6 OOP
Enfield Town & Palace Gates - BL to D 32 2
Epsom to Horsham A 30 4
Euston to Harrow & Wealdstone C 89 3
Exeter & Taunton Tramways B 32 4
Exeter to Barnstaple B 15 4
Exeter to Newton Abbot C 49 4
Exeter to Tavistock B 69 3
Exmouth - Branch Lines to B 00 6
F
Fairford - Branch Line to A 52 5
Falmouth, Helston & St. Ives - BL to C 74 5
Fareham to Salisbury A 67 3
Faversham to Dover B 05 7
Felixstowe & Aldeburgh - BL to D 20 9
Fenchurch Street to Barking C 20 6
Festiniog - 50 yrs of enterprise C 83 4
Festiniog in the Fifties B 68 5
Festiniog in the Sixties B 91 X
Finsbury Park to Alexandra Palace C 02 8
Frome to Bristol B 77 4
Fulwell - Trams, Trolleys & Buses D 11 X
G
Gloucester to Bristol D 35 7
Gloucester to Cardiff D 66 7
Gosport & Horndean Trys B 92 8
Gosport - Branch Lines around A 36 3
Great Yarmouth Tramways D 13 6
Greece Narrow Gauge D 72 1
Greenwich & Dartford Tramways B 14 6 OOP
Grimsby & Cleethorpes Trolleybuses D 86 1
Guildford to Redhill A 63 0 OOP
H
Hammersmith & Hounslow Trys C 33 8
Hampshire Narrow Gauge D 36 5
Hampshire Waterways A 84 3 OOP
Hampstead & Highgate Tramways B 53 7
Harrow to Watford D 14 4
Hastings to Ashford A 37 1
Hastings Tramways B 18 9
Hastings Trolleybuses B 81 2 OOP
Hawkhurst - Branch Line to A 66 5
Hayling - Branch Line to A 12 6
Haywards Heath to Seaford A 28 2
Henley, Windsor & Marlow - BL to C77 X
Hereford to Newport D 54 3
Hexham to CarlisleD 75 6
Hitchin to Peterborough D 07 1
Holborn & Finsbury Tramways B 79 0
Holborn Viaduct to Lewisham A 81 9
Horsham - Branch Lines to A 02 9
Huddersfield Trolleybuses C 92 3
Hull Tramways D60 8
Hull Trolleybuses D 24 1
Huntingdon - Branch Lines around A 93 2
I
Ilford & Barking Tramways B 61 8
Ilford to Shenfield C 97 4
Ilfracombe - Branch Line to B 21 9
Ilkeston & Glossop Tramways D 40 3
Industrial Rlys of the South East A 09 6
Ipswich to Saxmundham C 41 9
Ipswich Trolleybuses D 59 4
Isle of Wight Lines - 50 yrs C 12 5
K
Keighley Tramways & Trolleybuses D 83 7
Kent & East Sussex Waterways A 72 X
Kent Narrow Gauge C 45 1
Kent Seaways - Hoys to Hovercraft D 79 9
Kingsbridge - Branch Line to C 98 2
Kingston & Hounslow Loops A 83 5 OOP
Kingston & Wimbledon Tramways B 56 1
Kingswear - Branch Line to C 17 6
L
Lambourn - Branch Line to C 70 2
Launceston & Princetown - BL to C 19 2
Lewisham & Catford Tramways B 26 X OOP
Lewisham to Dartford A 92 4
Lines around Wimbledon B 75 8
Liverpool Street to Chingford D 01 2
Liverpool Street to Ilford C 34 6
Liverpool Tramways - Eastern C 04 4
Liverpool Tramways - Northern C 46 X
Liverpool Tramways - Southern C 23 0
London Bridge to Addiscombe B 20 0
London Bridge to East Croydon A 58 4
London Chatham & Dover Railway A 88 6
London Termini - Past and Proposed D 00 4
London to Portsmouth Waterways B 43 X
Longmoor - Branch Lines to A 41 X
Looe - Branch Line to C 22 2
Lyme Regis - Branch Line to A 45 2
Lynton - Branch Line to B 04 9
M
Maidstone & Chatham Tramways B 40 5
Maidstone Trolleybuses C 00 1 OOP
March - Branch Lines around B 09 X
Margate & Ramsgate Tramways C 52 4
Marylebone to Rickmansworth D49 7
Midhurst - Branch Lines around A 49 5
Midhurst - Branch Lines to A 01 0 OOP
Military Defence of West Sussex A 23 1
Military Signals, South Coast C 54 0
Minehead - Branch Line to A 80 0
Mitcham Junction Lines B 01 4
Mitchell & company C 59 1
Monmouthshire Eastern Valleys D 71 3
Moreton-in-Marsh to Worcester D 26 8
Moretonhampstead - BL to C 27 3
Mountain Ash to Neath D 80 2
N
Newbury to Westbury C 66 4
Newcastle to Hexham D 69 1
Newcastle Trolleybuses D 78 0
Newport (IOW) - Branch Lines to A 26 6
Newquay - Branch Lines to C 71 0
Newton Abbot to Plymouth C 60 5
Northern France Narrow Gauge C 75 3
North East German Narrow Gauge D 44 6
North Kent Tramways B 44 8
North London Line B 94 4
North Woolwich - BLs around C 65 6
Norwich Tramways C 40 0
Nottinghamshire & Derbyshire T/B D 63 2
Nottinghamshire & Derbyshire T/W D 53 5
O
Orpington to Tonbridge B 03 0 OOP
Oxford to Bletchley D57 8
Oxford to Moreton-in-Marsh D 15 2
P
Paddington to Ealing C 37 0
Paddington to Princes Risborough C 81 8
Padstow - Branch Line to B 54 5
Plymouth - BLs around B 98 7
Plymouth to St. Austell C 63 X
Pontypool to Mountain Ash D 65 9
Porthmadog 1954-94 - BL around B 31 6
Porthmadog to Blaenau B 50 2 OOP
Portmadoc 1923-46 - BL around B 13 8
Portsmouths Tramways B 72 3
Portsmouth to Southampton A 31 2
Portsmouth Trolleybuses C 73 7
Potters Bar to Cambridge D 70 5
Princes Risborough - Branch Lines to D 05 5
Princes Risborough to Banbury C 85 0
R
Railways to Victory C 16 8/7 OOP
Reading to Basingstoke B 27 8
Reading to Didcot C 79 6
Reading to Guildford A 47 9 OOP
Reading Tramways B 87 1
Reading Trolleybuses C 05 2
Redhill to Ashford A 73 8
Return to Blaenau 1970-82 C 64 8
Rickmansworth to Aylesbury D 61 6
Roman Roads of Hampshire D 67 5
Roman Roads of Surrey C 61 3
Roman Roads of Sussex C 48 6
Romneyrail C 32 X
Ryde to Ventnor A 19 3
S
Salisbury to Westbury B 39 1
Salisbury to Yeovil B 06 5 OOP
Saxmundham to Yarmouth C 69 9
Saxony Narrow Gauge D 47 0
Seaton & Eastbourne Tramways B 76 6 OOP
Seaton & Sidmouth - Branch Lines to A 95 9
Secret Sussex Resistance B 82 0
SECR Centenary album C 11 7
Selsey - Branch Line to A 04 5
Sheerness - Branch Lines around B 16 2
Shepherds Bush to Uxbridge T/Ws C 28 1
Shrewsbury - Branch Line to A 86 X
Sierra Leone Narrow Gauge D 28 4
Sittingbourne to Ramsgate A 90 8
Slough to Newbury C 56 7
Solent - Creeks, Crafts & Cargoes D 52 7
Southamptons Tramways B 33 2
Southampton to Bournemouth A 42 8
Southend-on-Sea Tramways B 28 6
Southern France Narrow Gauge C 47 8
Southwark & Deptford Tramways B 38 3
Southwold - Branch Line to A 15 0
South Eastern & Chatham Railways C 08
South London Line B 46 4
South London Tramways 1903-33 D 10 1
St. Albans to Bedford D 08 X
St. Austell to Penzance C 67 2
St. Pancras to Barking D 68 3
St. Pancras to St. Albans C 78 8
Stamford Hill Tramways B 85 5
Steaming through Cornwall B 30 8 OOP
Steaming through Kent A 13 4 OOP
Steaming through the Isle of Wight A 56 8
Steaming through West Hants A 69 X
Stratford upon avon to Birmingham D 77
Stratford upon Avon to Cheltenham C 25
Strood to Paddock Wood B 12 X OOP
Surrey Home Guard C 57 5
Surrey Narrow Gauge C 87 7
Surrey Waterways A 51 7 OOP
Sussex Home Guard C 24 9
Sussex Narrow Gauge C 68 0
Sussex Shipping Sail, Steam & Motor D 2
Swanley to Ashford B 45 6
Swindon to Bristol C 96 6
Swindon to Gloucester D46 2
Swindon to Newport D 30 6
Swiss Narrow Gauge C 94 X
T
Talyllyn - 50 years C 39 7
Taunton to Barnstaple B 60 X
Taunton to Exeter C 82 6
Tavistock to Plymouth B 88 X
Tees-side Trolleybuses D 58 6
Tenterden - Branch Line to A 21 5
Thanet's Tramways B 11 1 OOP
Three Bridges to Brighton A 35 5
Tilbury Loop C 86 9
Tiverton - Branch Lines around C 62 1
Tivetshall to Beccles D 41 1
Tonbridge to Hastings A 44 4
Torrington - Branch Lines to B 37 5
Tunbridge Wells - Branch Lines to A 32 0
Twickenham & Kingston Trys C 35 4
Two-Foot Gauge Survivors C 21 4 OOP
U
Upwell - Branch Line to B 64 2
V
Victoria & Lambeth Tramways B 49 9
Victoria to Bromley South A 98 3
Victoria to East Croydon A 40 1 OOP
Vivarais C 31 1 OOP
W
Walthamstow & Leyton Tramways B 65 0
Waltham Cross & Edmonton Trys C 07 9
Wandsworth & Battersea Tramways B 63
Wantage - Branch Line to D 25 X
Wareham to Swanage - 50 yrs D 09 8
War on the Line A 10 X
War on the Line VIDEO + 88 0
Waterloo to Windsor A 54 1
Waterloo to Woking A 38 X
Watford to Leighton Buzzard D 45 4
Wenford Bridge to Fowey C 09 5
Westbury to Bath B 55 3
Westbury to Taunton C 76 1
West Cornwall Mineral Railways D 48 9
West Croydon to Epsom B 08 1
West London - Branch Lines of C 50 8
West London Line B 84 7
West Sussex Waterways A 24 X OOP
West Wiltshire - Branch Lines of D 12 8
Weymouth - Branch Lines around A 65 7
Willesden Junction to Richmond B 71 5
Wimbledon to Beckenham C 58 3
Wimbledon to Epsom B 62 6
Wimborne - Branch Lines around A 97 5
Wisbech - Branch Lines around C 01 X
Wisbech 1800-1901 C 93 1
Woking to Alton A 59 2
Woking to Portsmouth A 25 8
Woking to Southampton A 55 X
Wolverhampton Trolleybuses D 85 3
Woolwich & Dartford Trolleys B 66 9
Worcester to Hereford D 38 1
Worthing to Chichester A 06 1
Y
Yeovil - 50 yrs change C 38 9
Yeovil to Dorchester A 76 2 OOP
Yeovil to Exeter A 91 6
York Tramways & Trolleybuses D 82 9